ESSENTIAL GOLF

Everything you need to know

And how to learn it!

Second Edition

ESSENTIAL GOLF

Everything you need to know
And how to learn it!

Second Edition

John Dunigan

GOLF BETTER PRODUCTIONS
West Chester, Pa

ESSENTIAL

GOLF

Library of Congress Catalog Card Number:
  Dunigan, John, 1965-
  Essential Golf : Everything you need to know. *And* how to learn it! By John
  Dunigan.—2nd ed.
ISBN 0-9669375-0-3
LCCN 98-96930 1998
  1. Golf (golf swing)

GOLF BETTER PRODUCTIONS

Welcome to GOLF BETTER PRODUCTIONS.

Launched in 1998, GOLF BETTER PRODUCTIONS was founded to help educate golfers in their quest to learn or relearn the game we love so much.

Our mission is simple. We want to see the national average golf score improve from its rather dismal 100—something that hasn't happened in over twenty years. Golfers are not improving, it's that simple. GOLF BETTER PRODUCTIONS seeks to change that painful reality by publishing instructional material that really works. We're committed to giving you the information you absolutely must master to play this game well. Our premise is that you are much better than you think. You just need more accurate, clear and concise instruction, and to know how to learn it.

GOLF BETTER PRODUCTIONS—*Dedicated to helping golfers GOLF BETTER!*

What people are saying about
ESSENTIAL GOLF

"An ideal 'how to' book for beginning golfers."

John Dunigan's Essential Golf is a complete introduction to the sport and teaches the reader not only what to learn about golf, but how to best go about learning it. Dunigan provides a clear and illustrated explanation of the key and essential elements of the game including putting, chipping, pitching, the full swing, ball flight, and more. ESSENTIAL GOLF is enhanced with drills and more than 260 photos showing the reader clearly and informatively what they must do in each golfing circumstance in order to play the game well. A "must" for all novice golfers, Essential Golf has much of value to recommend it to those who have been away from the game and are returning to it, as well as to anyone seeking to improve their performance on the golf course. *Jim Cox, Midwest Book Review*

"I read your book and immediately took ten strokes off my game." *Joe Butcher,* Syracuse, NY

"Using the concepts and drills in ESSENTIAL GOLF, I lowered my handicap from 13 to 8 in just three months!" *Eugene Makar, President BWI-Ltd.*

"A true classic! If you must own only one golf instruction book, make this the one!" *Daniel Ozelis, retired CEO*

"I have read ESSENTIAL GOLF and thought so highly of it that I have purchased copies for friend's Christmas gifts." *Dr. Thomas Celello, MD PA*

"I love the approach you use to build a swing step by step, focusing on simple, repeatable swing thoughts. I have read quite a bit and have taken numerous lessons, but I just seemed to clog up my head with conflicting and confusing information with little improvement. I really feel like I now have a good concept of the swing and that I am on the verge of really improving my game. My kids and wife think I'm nuts for always swinging the club in the house, but I'm psyched!" *Jim Salmon, 25 handicap*

"Absolutely one of the best golf books I've ever read. I have an extensive collection of instruction books at home, and this one ranks right up there with the best of them! *Spencer A. Graham III, PGA Professional*

From amazon.com

Easiest Swing Model to learn!
"After spending many dollars on various golf schools, I find this presentation of the golf swing one of the easiest to understand, visualize and execute. The lessons on the short game had an immediate impact on how I played. For the first time I have a

model to use when practicing my swing. I am enjoying the drills and know I am improving. Thanks, John."

"As a person who loves to play golf but cannot get out to play but once or twice a month, this book provides great instruction to help me monitor my own game."

"Thanks for the easy-to-read instruction and terrific drills. It's about time someone made sense of the game for me after years of playing. I'm starting my kids the "ES-SENTIAL GOLF" way."

"This book makes it easy to understand the game and shows you how and why your ball does what it does. The illustrations are important to the beginner and help get you on the right track."

An "employee favorite" at amazon.com

Acknowledgments

To my golf students. Because of you, this book is possible. You have taught me far more than I can say. In fact, I'm not really sure who the teacher is.

I wish to thank Dick Dubroff of FINAL FOCUS in Wilmington, De. for his superb work on the cover photos and full swing sequence photos.

Special thanks go to Davis Sezna from Hartefeld National Golf Course in Avondale, Pa., to Rod and Mike King at Mocassin Run Golf Club in Atglen, Pa. and Alan Liddicote at Frog Hollow Golf Course in Middletown, De. for allowing us to take our photographs on their fine golf courses.

My teaching has been significantly influenced by so many people that it's difficult to list them all. I feel compelled to mention these people because I am forever in debt to them. It would be misleading, not to mention dishonest, for me to lead you to believe that I had no help in learning what I know.

Mike Bender is one of the most knowledgeable people in the world on the golf swing. He helped me considerably with my own swing while I was competing. Chuck Hogan has been a major influence on the way I teach golf. His work has opened my mind and forced me to constantly evaluate what I teach and how I teach it. I've watched Craig Shankland give more golf clinics than I can count; he's wonderful to watch at work. Dave Pelz's study of the short game has probably influenced every golfer in the world, whether they know it or not. Lynn Marriot, whom I've met through the LPGA Urban Youth Golf Program, is another brilliant teacher from whom I've learned. Anything you can get your hands on by Joseph Chilton Pearce will change your life. The willingness of these people to share what they know with us is impressive and all too rare in this competitive world. I'd like to thank these folks for making golf a better game and for making the world a better place.

I'd like to thank all my friends for their support and aid with editing and photography. To Joe Schulte, Samantha Keith, Daniel Ozelis, Billy Dickinson, John Gledhill Jr., Bill Tansey, Gene Makar, Alex Jenkins, Roger London and Andrew VonDeak: Thank you for your time, energy, and immense help, I could not have done it without you. And to my wife, Francine, thank you for allowing me to spend countless hours writing while the yard turned into a jungle. Baby, you're the greatest!

Dedication

This book is for you, Mom.

You always told me I could do anything I wanted to.

Thanks for putting up with me all those years when I thought

I knew all the answers.

Why you need this book

If you want to learn or improve your golf, you must not only know *what* to do, more importantly, you need to know *how to learn* what to do so that you avoid or change the bad habits that make golf more difficult than it really is.

If you are a new golfer, don't even think of starting out without some guidance. On your own, this game may take you forever to learn, but it doesn't have to happen like that.

If you have been golfing for some time, you might be pretty frustrated with golf. Listen. The average golf score has not improved in over twenty years, largely because golf has been taught improperly, and learned even worse. This book will clear up some of the misinformation that has made golf such a mystery to the average golfer. Well, there is no magic involved. The application of some basic principles is what the game is about. Unfortunately, those basic principles are often misunderstood and misinterpreted, if not avoided completely. This book makes sense out of the non-sense.

Golf is not really all that difficult, but it is a bit of a struggle to learn all that there is to know. However, the guided struggle is far better than the blind struggle. This book is your guide to good golf.

My plan is to give you a complete understanding of golf, so that you can become your own coach. I wrote this book precisely because I think you can play this game well *if* you learn it correctly. I am going to teach you exactly what you need to know, and I'm going to tell you exactly how to learn it. All you have to do is follow instructions.

This book is written mainly for the beginning to advanced intermediate golfer in search of a better way to learn, practice, and play the game. If your score is above 90, this book is for you. If you're trying to break 80, the drills inside will help you get there fast. If you are frustrated, you will find what you need to make golf fun again. You will find this instruction simple, clear and very effective, but don't kid yourself: you will have to apply yourself to learn it.

This improved edition is even better than the first (which I've heard is quite good!) because, to be honest, I keep learning, just like you. I've got many new additions which will help you learn even faster than with the first edition. You'll quickly improve your golf and enjoy the process.

How to use this book

This book is designed as your guide, so keep your guide with you when you practice. I have written for the right-handed golfer, so if you are left handed, reverse the rights and lefts throughout. First of all, study the pictures and try to absorb them into your mind. Close your eyes after studying them for a while. Can you see the pictures in your mind's eye? All learning occurs through a model, so you need to get clear pictures in your head to serve as your model before you attempt to learn the movements. If you are not clear in your mind, your mind certainly can't tell your body what to do.

Once you have a crystal clear picture in your head, then pick up the club. Begin very slowly and *without a ball*, try to match the pictures. Smooth out the motion until you can flow through the swing without a hitch. Begin to feel how the motion is designed to send your energy, through the club head, toward the target. Think, "this is what it feels like to swing to the target." Put a ball down and make the same swing toward the target, and just let the ball get in the way. Make no effort to hit the ball. Simply make your swing until you find the ball with it. Watch out for *trying* to hit the ball: You can ruin your swing real fast. I suggest that you go very slowly when you first put a ball down and concentrate totally on making the correct swing, collecting the ball along the way. If you hit the ball, that's fine. If you don't, that's fine too. Don't worry about contact, it'll come with experience and repetition.

You have to know your swing in your mind first, and then let your mind teach it to your body. I guarantee that you will be able to teach yourself better if you go slowly. As your hands learn where to go, you will become increasingly comfortable with, and proficient at, the motion. As you have to work less to make the right motion, you will naturally increase your speed. Don't rush the speed. You'll learn bad habits and then you'll have to come see me, and that's a lot more expensive than this book.

When your mechanics are set (which you can do at home), go to the range or putting green, book in hand, and start on the drills. Begin the process of educating your hands, and then go *PLAY GOLF*. Get feedback from the golf course on where you need improvement and consult the book for how to proceed. It's all here. Go to it.

A note from the author

Congratulations, you have just purchased the only golf instruction book you will ever need. Many golfers will lead you to believe that golf is unbearably difficult and frustrating. Well, it's not *easy*, but if you use the information contained in these pages, you will understand the mechanics of the full swing, the short game, specialty shots, and the mental game, *and* you will learn a method of practicing that will make golf much easier for you and help you shoot lower scores almost immediately.

I wrote this book because I am dismayed that, despite the wealth of instructional material out there, golfers still don't understand how golf works. The national average golf score hasn't improved in just about forever, clearly illustrating the fact that an awful lot of golfers are not improving. Traditional instruction materials somehow manage to leave out the critical elements of golf that you really need to know. I wrote this book to teach you those elements. You need to know what's right, rather than try to guess what's wrong. Think about this: 80% of all golfers slice the ball. I believe that the reason for that is that they are doing just what they have been taught. Golfers also make the game more difficult by practicing in a way that almost ensures that they don't improve. This book is here to teach you what to practice and how to practice correctly so that you do improve.

Golfers are frustrated by instruction that has gotten far too complex and difficult for the average player to understand, let alone master. Sometimes, what is appropriate for the touring pro is simply much too difficult for the average person to learn. When is the last time you hit five or six hundred balls a day for a few *years*? I intend to make golf much simpler for you. You'll get the most out of whatever practice time you have.

Listen. Golf is not as difficult as you think. Playing the game for a living is difficult. I've tried that, and let me tell you it's *tough*. But playing respectably and continually improving your game is pretty easy, if you have the patience to learn correctly. Playing good golf is *much* easier if you have the following:

- Clear pictures in your mind that will serve as models for the short game and the full swing mechanics you will need to play golf.

- A method of practicing that ensures you become the model.

- An understanding of what makes a ball fly the way it does.

- A complete learning program that covers all aspects of the game, both mental and physical, so that you learn not only the mechanics of golf, but also how to score.

ESSENTIAL GOLF gives you all that and more.

Although you will find a revolutionary approach to the full swing in this book, I want to make it clear that the full swing is only a small part of golf. Golf is about getting the ball in the hole in the least number of strokes possible, therefore, *ESSEN-TIAL GOLF* also includes what you *must* know about putting, chipping, pitching and sand play. You will be able to build a complete game with this book as your guide.

Part of the problem with golf is that you don't know *what* to learn in the first place. There is so much instructional material out there it's scary, and the content of the material varies wildly in an often contradictory way that leads to total confusion for people trying to learn. I'm here to end the confusion.

THE MODEL

All learning occurs through a model. You could not write the letter "A" without a model of an "A" in your mind. You *need* a model. If you are like most golfers, you have several opposing ideas (models) about the golf swing. Rather than becoming a student of the game, with more technical knowledge than ability to use it, you need to stick to one model until you learn it, and ignore all others. By embracing a model and working toward it, you rid yourself of the paralyzing indecision most golfers face on every shot: "Which swing should I use this time?" It will help to know that the full swing model in this book is as close to the perfect swing as you can get.

THE SWING—NOT THE BALL

The second part of your problem is that you must practice correctly so that you learn the correct mechanics. Most golfers, and I don't mean just the bad ones, do not know how to practice well. Far too many golfers approach golf the wrong way right from the start. You probably did the same thing most golfers do: Head straight to the range with no idea of what to do and smashed balls as hard as you could until you either ran out of balls or quit from frustration. The problem is that darned ball. If you put the ball in the way too soon, you'll try to hit it. Yes, I meant to say that! Rather than make a swing designed to send the ball to a target, you'll make a swing designed to hit the ball. Those two swings are very different. The swing designed to hit the ball doesn't go toward the target. Want the ball to go to the target? Well a good place to start is to swing toward it!

FEEL IS NOT REAL

So many golfers rely only on their sense of feel to tell them that their mechanics are correct. If it feels good, it must be good, right? Wrong. Way wrong! Don't mistake the feel of good contact with a good swing. The truth is, you may *think* that you are making the right move, but unless you have some kind of feedback (video is the best), you really don't have any idea what you are actually doing. Any swing can make good contact. A *good* swing sends the ball to the target. You must get the mechanics correct first, and then learn how those mechanics feel or you'll most certainly learn incorrectly. Mechanics first, feel later. Please don't forget that!

EVALUATE WHAT YOU'RE WORKING ON

Golfers also make the vital mistake of working on one thing and then evaluating something entirely different. You may have done the same. There you are on the range, working on your swing, but instead of evaluating your swing itself, you intently watch the ball fly in order to determine whether you made the right swing. It's not fair to you, and it's no way to learn.

The last part of your problem may be that you have not committed yourself to learning the game. Golf is not like tennis. In tennis, you can jump on the court and, within a short amount of time, get the ball going back and forth well enough to have a blast. Not so in golf. You are going to have to pay some dues first. The good news is that if you learn correctly the first time, you can seriously shorten the dues paying period. But you are definitely not going to escape it altogether.

This book is designed to be a complete guide to learning golf. Everything that you will find in these pages is essential. No quick fixes or unnecessary complications, just the fundamentals. That's where the name comes from. Further, I don't just tell you to do something, I teach you *how* to learn it. Although I may contradict some old, standard methods of teaching (thank goodness), you will find that what I teach you makes perfect common sense and, more importantly, that *you can do it*. You will get a model for every part of the game; drills to help you learn; and you will learn how to bring your new skills to the golf course. In other words, you will get a complete learning package. This book is all you need.

Ask yourself these questions: Are you getting better? Are you happy with your progress? Do you understand golf? Do you know what you are supposed to look like? Do you know what makes the ball do what it does? Do you get the most out of your practice time? Chances are that if you picked up this book, you need some help. Help is here.

I don't think there is another book out there that is as complete or as thorough in its instruction. I sincerely believe that this book will be of great value to you. If you have questions or comments, visit us on the web at www.golfbetterproductions.com or send email to john@golfbetterproductions.com or write John Dunigan at Golf Better Productions 317 West Biddle St. Suite 1A West Chester Pa. 19380.

Happy Learning,

John Dunigan
West Chester, Pa.

Contents

WHY YOU NEED THIS BOOK X

HOW TO USE THIS BOOK........................XI

A NOTE FROM THE AUTHOR XII

INTRODUCTION 19

The only way to improve your golf 19

Common Golf Misconceptions 20

Right Practice 22

Before you swing 24

Important terms 27

SECTION 1 THE SHORT GAME 31

PUTTING 33

Holding the Putter 34

Putting Setup 35

The Iron Triangle 36

The Iron Triangle Putt 37

The Push 38

The Putting Track 39

Watch out for these mistakes 41

The Pre-Shot Routine, Part 1 42

Aiming Exercise 44

Short but Sweet 45

Reading Greens 46

Three Ball 48

The Ladder 49

Around the World 50

Four Corners 51

The Twenty Footer 52

CHIPPING 55

The Full Swing Hold 56

Chipping Setup 60

The Iron Triangle Chip 62

The Long Club 63

Downward Contact 64

Pick a Spot 65

Up and Down 66

Watch out for these mistakes 67

PITCHING 69

Address Position 70

Do these drills slowly and perfectly!!! 73
The Push 74
Full swing address and pitching address 76
Get the swing right first! 77
The Iron Triangle Pitch 78
The Three Quarter Backswing 80
The Three Quarter Pitch 82
Keys to the Three Quarter Pitch 84
Make your practice count 85
Getting the ball to the target 86
Watch out for these mistakes 87

SECTION 2 THE LONG GAME 89

THE FULL BACKSWING 91

The importance of a model 92
7 Steps to good golf 93
The Turn 94
The Level Turn 96
 The Address Position Turn 98
The Belly Button Turn 99
The Full Backswing 100
At the Top 101
Watch out for these mistakes 102

THE DOWNSWING 103

The Arc of Approach 104
Back, Down, and Forward 105
The Swing Plane Model 106
The Plane Truth 108
The Swing Circle, Part 1 110
The Difference between Down and Out...................111
The Swing Circle, Part 2 112
The Angle of Attack 113
Downswing Keys 114
Power Storage and Release 116
The Punch Shot 118
The Finish 120
The Full Swing 122
The four keys to the swing 130
Watch out for this mistake 134

FULL SWING DRILLS 137

Gradual Acceleration 138
The Obstacle Course 140
The Three Followthroughs 142
The Level Swing 144
The Foot High Swing..146

The Swinging Start 148
Feet Together 149
Right Foot Out 150
Left Foot Out 151
Right Hand Only 152

SECTION 3 PRACTICING AND PLAYING 153

PRACTICING GOLF 155

What are all those clubs for, anyway? 156
Posture 158
Ball Location 159
Approaching the ball and the waggle 160
Contact! 161
The right clubs for you! 162
Ball Flight Control 163
Ball Flight Laws Quiz 165
Educated Hands 167
How to practice golf 168
Pre-Shot Routine, Part 2 170
Recommended Practice Routine 171
Rhythm and Tempo 174

DIFFERENT LIES 175

Downhill 176
Uphill 177
Sidehill, above your feet 178
Sidehill, below your feet 178
Deep Rough 179
Short Rough 179
Tight Lies 180
In a Divot 180
Sand Play 181
The Slider 182
The Rake Line 183
Where to enter the sand 184
The Explosion 185
Fairway Bunkers 186

PLAYING GOLF 187

Etiquette 188
Golf: the mind game 193

TROUBLESHOOTING 201

Introduction

THE ONLY WAY TO IMPROVE YOUR GOLF

Improving your golf game is all in your head. Saying you want to learn or improve is the easy part. The hard part is backing up your words with commitment. You must realize that, in the beginning, you will have to grind through the initiation period that all of us have had to go through. You don't just start out good at this game. You have to earn it. There are no natural golfers, the good ones just look natural because they have stuck with it through the inevitable ups and downs that make this game such a challenge. Realize now that no one has ever mastered the game. The best players in the world have all had times when they felt they could do no wrong and times when they felt the opposite. The key is to hang in there when you seem to be going backward, because you are not far from leaping forward. Anyone can play this game. You don't need fantastic natural talent. What you really need are persistence and patience.

Learn to *PLAY GOLF*. That's the whole point of this book. Get fascinated by the process of golfing and what makes a ball do what it does. It's not that difficult. You can do it. You just have to learn and put to use a few fundamental motions and you're on your way. Go slowly. Get the mechanics down first. Then add the ball. I can't say that enough.

You will have to discipline yourself to practice correctly. What is good practice? Good practice entails knowing *what* to practice, *why* to practice it and *how* to practice it. You must concentrate on exactly what you are working on, whether it is your swing mechanics or your ball flight, and then evaluate only what you are working on. Then you must be able to apply your knowledge on the golf course in all types of situations and under all sorts of conditions.

BE PATIENT! This is going to take some time. There is just *so much* to learn. The fundamentals are actually easy, but the variety of shots you need to play the game requires quite a lot of learning before you can "just do it." That's OK. Just take your time. Realize that you are headed in the right direction, and you'll be fine.

COMMON GOLF MISCONCEPTIONS

YOU CAN LEARN OR MAKE CHANGES WHILE SWINGING THE CLUB AT FULL SPEED.

Feel is not real. At full speed, you may *feel* that you are making a new move, but the reality is that you will do the same old move *thinking* it's the new move. Full speed happens too fast, so whatever habits you have will show up when you go full speed. I see it all the time. Even my own students will sometimes practice only at full speed between lessons and not improve as much as they could have. The inevitable result is that the next lesson is the same as the last one.

I constantly implore my students to slow down so that the club does not move faster than they can control. Your mind must be fully aware of what's moving when and where the club is throughout the motion. I have my students say out loud the keys to their swing *as they go through them* to create and increase their awareness of their motion. This approach should be taken for all stroke mechanics in this book. The rapid progress my students make when they practice slowly never ceases to amazes me.

START THE FORWARD SWING BY TURNING EITHER YOUR HIPS OR SHOULDERS.

Earlier, I mentioned that 80% of the world's golfers slice the ball. The reason can be directly traced to the mistaken notion that some form of body turn should start the forward swing. The Full Swing chapter will show you very clearly that if you do start the forward swing with your body, your hands will follow your body and move away from, rather than toward, the swing plane. The result will be that your club will not swing toward the target as it moves through impact. It will swing to the left of the target unless you somehow manage to correct yourself in mid-swing, which is highly unlikely. Unfortunately, this misconception is still widely taught.

POWER COMES FROM YOUR LEGS, HIPS OR BODY.

Believe it or not, the number one power generator in the golf swing is your right arm, for right handed golfers. Using a small computer to measure club head speed, I hit five iron shots with my normal effort swing. My club head speed was consistently around 90 m.p.h.. Then I hit the same club holding it in only my right hand. My club head speed was consistently around 73 m.p.h.. *With one hand!* That means that *eighty- one percent* of my club head speed comes from my right arm/hand. Furthermore, I hit my seven iron 160 yards with my normal swing. With only my right hand on the club, I hit it about 130 yards. Interesting, huh?

WEIGHT SHIFT ADDS DISTANCE TO YOUR GOLF SHOTS.

Club head speed and the angle of attack are the most important determinants of distance. I wanted to find out the relationship between weight shift and club head speed, so I spent three hours on a friend's golf computer that measured weight shift, club head speed, club path and club face angle. I hit drivers, varying the amount of weight shift (from one foot to the other) from just about zero (no change from address), up to seventy percent on the backswing, to seventy percent on the forward swing (at impact that is, not at the finish). What I found was that the difference in club head speed between zero weight shift and seventy percent weight shift was approximately *one mile per hour*. One mile per hour is worth only about 2.33 yards, which I find to be insignificant. The real news is that the more I shifted my weight, the farther off line my club path and face angle were, creating amazingly less control with very little additional distance. That's not a wise trade-off.

KEEP YOUR HEAD STILL.

This is a dangerous misconception because if you attempt to keep your head perfectly still, you will not be able to make a proper backswing turn, and that will set you up for failure right from the start. Allow your head to turn a little to the right and move as much as two inches to the right as you make your backswing. The important thing is to make sure that you don't straighten up your spine angle as you swing, not that you keep your head still.

I PICKED MY HEAD UP.

I can't tell you how many times I have heard golfers say exactly this after missing the ball completely or rolling it along the ground. Picking your head up is almost never the problem here. The way to miss or roll a shot is to stand up as you make the backswing, or bend your arms as you swing the club forward through impact.

KEEP YOUR HANDS PASSIVE, AND LET YOUR BODY CONTROL THE CLUB.

The club isn't stuck to your belly button, it's stuck to your hands. Need I say more?

PULL WITH YOUR LEFT HAND AND KEEP YOUR RIGHT HAND OUT OF THE SWING.

Are you left-handed or right-handed? If you're left-handed, play left-handed. If you're right-handed, play right-handed. Doesn't that make sense?

HOLD THE ANGLE, DELAY THE HIT, OR DON'T CAST THE CLUB.

These ideas all refer to the release of power during the swing. They have confused golfers for years, and they are all simply the result of deceleration. All you need to do is accelerate *through impact* (not just at the ball) and you'll have nothing to worry about.

Be careful what you listen to. This game is much simpler than most golfers have been led to believe. When someone tries to give you advice, ask them two questions: "What do you shoot?" and "Why do you want me to do that?" If you don't get sensible answers to either question, run away—fast.

Right Practice

We all want to be better immediately, but that's not gonna happen. What is possible is that if you practice correctly and do your homework, you can quickly own a swing to be proud of and be well on your way to hitting controlled, powerful shots. However, that's not all there is to golf, you must have a good short game. If you work on your short game as shown in this book, you will continually improve your ability to get the ball in the hole. Of course, as with anything, how fast you improve depends upon the quality and frequency of your practice. Here are a few Rules of Right Practice which you would do well to follow.

Rule #1 Have fun!

Golf is a game, and games are for fun. Right? So have fun. Have fun learning and experimenting with all the facets of the game. Have fun making mistakes. Mistakes are good because they point out weaknesses in your game which, when improved, will make you a better golfer. Walk whenever you can and have fun getting exercise among the beautiful scenery.

Rule #2 Be nice to yourself.

I'm serious. Be your own best friend. Talk to yourself in a nurturing, helpful, positive way. Have you ever called yourself stupid for hitting a bad shot? Don't. Maintain your self-esteem and your sense of humor. It *is* just a game, isn't it?

Rule #3 Slow down and forget about contact.

If you want to improve your swing, concentrate on your swing, not contact. If the swing is not there first, contact could be a real problem. If you attempt to focus on both swing and contact at the same time, you will get neither, and that's no fun. Practice your swing and make sure it's correct. At first, you will have to slow way down to make a good swing, and that's a good thing. Your brain will learn whatever you teach it, whether you go fast or slow. So if you want to learn the correct swing, practice slowly and perfectly, and gradually add speed later. Contact is easy. When your swing is ready, contact will be a matter of simple adjustment.

Rule #4 Remove the word "bad" from your vocabulary.

Please do not judge undesirable results as bad. There is no failure, only feedback. You swing, the ball goes somewhere, you say "Hmm, interesting," and you try again. For instance, if you make a swing and determine that you made a club path error, instantly forget the shot, and take a couple of practice swings with the perfect club path to remind yourself of what you wanted to do. Immediately replace an errant swing with the right swing and tell yourself "That's the swing!" That's a whole lot more fun than beating yourself up or trying to figure out what you did wrong.

You need to enjoy your good shots. Get psyched about them. That which you give more emotion to becomes more strongly imprinted in your mind, so store only the results you want to repeat. Every time you hit a good shot, give yourself a big smile and congratulate yourself. Don't just assume that you *should* hit 'em that way. Most players brush aside their good shots and give all their emotion to the bad ones. Now that doesn't make any sense, does it?

RULE #5 TRY AND TRY AGAIN.

Once you are ready to introduce the ball, watch your shots closely until the ball stops rolling. Become very interested in where the ball goes. Once you learn to swing well, you have to "trial and error it" until you are able to make good contact, swing the club in the right direction or putt or chip the ball the right distance. It's easy. Adjust. Do not make the same mistake over and over again. You won't have fun, and you won't learn as fast.

RULE #6 USE SOME FORM OF FEEDBACK.

When you are working on your full swing, you must have a feedback mechanism so that you can be certain you are practicing correctly. Do not trust your feel, your feel is just not accurate. If you have a video camera, use it often. You will learn your swing in a matter of weeks if you spend at least fifteen minutes per day practicing correctly. Don't practice making mistakes, you might get good at it!

BEFORE YOU SWING

First you'll need some clubs. For now, a putter and a sand wedge or pitching wedge will do, but in a short while, you will need clubs that fit you well. Here are my *general* guidelines: Men taller than six feet-one may need longer than standard, men's clubs. Women with good hand and arm strength who are five feet-eight or taller probably should use men's standard length clubs. Women under five feet-seven may need ladies length clubs. Women around five feet and under may need petite clubs.

Juniors should have either ladies clubs (for taller youngsters), or their own junior clubs. Junior clubs have lighter shafts and club heads than adult clubs that have been cut down, making them easier to swing. Use a junior set if possible. Your children will have more success hitting the ball, and success makes golf more fun. Actually, that goes for golfers of all ages, doesn't it?

It is important to have clubs which fit your size and swing. You will find it easier to hit good shots. Please have a PGA Professional or knowledgeable club-fitter set you up with the right shaft length and flex, the correct grip size, and the proper lie angle. You'll be happy you did.

ON GOLF CLUBS

Nowadays, it is almost impossible to buy a new set of "bad" irons. The golf industry has reached a state where iron head technology is about as good as it can get. For about $200, you can buy an excellent set of irons that will be almost, if not just, as good as a $700 or $800 set. The key is getting clubs that fit *you*.

Driver technology is still improving, but I do not see how club manufacturers are going to improve much at all on the oversized, titanium drivers that are available now. I do believe that the titanium drivers are the best drivers ever offered (note that the best players in the world overwhelmingly use titanium). The benefit, however, is not raw distance. Although titanium *can* send the ball a little farther if you hit it just right, don't bet the house on your new driver making you the longest hitter at your club. What you get with titanium is a bigger "effective hitting surface," not a bigger "sweetspot." Basically, the real difference between today's drivers and the old ones is that your mis-hits will go straighter, and therefore they will *play* as if you hit them longer. But, of course, golf is a game of minimizing the severity of your missed shots, and your misses will be better using an oversized titanium driver.

To make things a little more confusing, I prefer smaller headed, not-necessarily-titanium, fairway woods because they are easier to hit from the rough and other imperfect lies. Bigger heads are a little less manageable in difficult lies, but they're great when the ball's on a tee.

THE GRAPHITE QUESTION

Do you need graphite shafts? You will be hard pressed to find steel shafted drivers and fairway woods these days. Why are graphite shafts so popular? It's the *promise* of greater distance. Graphite is lighter that steel, therefore anyone will be able to generate more club head speed with graphite as opposed to steel. Also, due to their light weight, graphite shafts can be made longer than steel shafts, adding still more club head speed. In fact, the main reason why today's new drivers hit the ball farther than ever is that their shafts are considerably longer than those made just a few years ago. It's not really the material out of which the club head is made at all.

It sounds like graphite is great, doesn't it? Well, there are drawbacks. First of all, longer shafted clubs are more difficult to control (golfers are driving the ball farther into the woods than ever). Also, graphite twists more at impact than steel, causing less accuracy, particularly on mis-hits. The word "torque" refers to the club shaft's resistance to twisting. The greater a shaft's torque, the more it twists. The club head is attached to the shaft, and so when the shaft twists, the club head will follow suit, and that can't be good.

So what am I torquing about? (sorry, I couldn't resist). If you swing the club slowly, the lightness of graphite shafts may help you get a little more club head speed, but if you swing the club quickly, perhaps at club head speeds of eighty m.p.h. or more with a five iron, the same graphite shaft will twist (at the most critical moment in the golf swing; impact) significantly more than a steel shaft, possibly sending the ball farther off line than it might have gone. Steel shafts are also easier to match than graphite, so steel shafted irons will perform more consistently through the set than graphite shafted irons. For these reasons, I feel very confident telling you that steel shafts play better than graphite, at least in the irons.

The positive statements I can make for using graphite are that it is lighter and perhaps a little easier to swing and it dampens vibration more than steel, making it more suitable for players who either lack swing speed, or have elbow or other arm problems that could be exacerbated by shock and vibration at impact. Nowadays, you can buy steel shafts with vibration dampening inserts that actually damp more vibration than graphite. As far as woods go, however, since you will find it very difficult to find steel shafted woods, you will have to search for woods that come with low torque shafts. Additionally, it may not be as difficult to find reasonably similar wood shafts because you'll probably have only a Driver, 3 Wood and 5 Wood in your bag, as opposed to nine or ten irons. Interestingly, really good graphite shafts are designed to perform just like steel, but you're going to pay a *lot* more for the graphite shaft: Top of the line graphite shafts start at about $75. I have one that cost $200, just for the shaft. I don't even use it. I hit my steel shafted driver considerably straighter and it cost me only $25—including installation. How about that? Incidentally, if you have a driver that you like but don't hit well, you may just need a new shaft, not a whole new driver. Go to a facility where you can try out several shafts and hit them all until you find the one that works best.

BUYING CLUBS

Listen. If you are just starting out in golf, it makes very little sense to go out and spend $800 on a set of irons and then spend another $300 or so *each* for woods. In the first place, you are going to give whatever clubs you buy quite a beating in your first year of golf, and in the second place, you almost certainly could not tell the difference between a $300 set of irons and an $800 set anyway. My point is, save your money (for now) and get stainless steel irons with steel shafts and, after you master the material in this book, get the clubs fit to you. Proper fitting may include having the club heads bent into the correct "lie" for your swing, (don't worry about bending the clubs, it's very common). You will want to own your swing mechanics before you get your clubs fit to you. Otherwise, you may need to have them altered again.

You do not have to buy a titanium driver right away. Remember, you are going to have to learn to make good contact through trial and error. It makes more sense to trial and error it with less expensive clubs. After you get your swing ironed out and make good contact regularly, then you may want to upgrade to titanium. You don't want to pay $350 for one club and then ruin it, do you? If money is not important, good for you. You can ignore the above.

Beware empty promises and marketing gimmicks

I'd like to think that all advertisements are truthful, but... You have to watch out for promises about the magic a new set of clubs will work for you. You already know what I think about shafts, but don't forget what I said about club heads: Whatever you get these days is going to be very similar to every other set out there. Once you get clubs that fit you, they will *all* perform very much alike.

Now don't go thinking that some club is going to transform your game. That's ridiculous. You can't buy a golf game. All you can do is buy the best equipment you can afford, and make sure it fits you. Swinging the thing is up to you.

I remember an unsatisfied customer who demanded his money back because his new wedge hit the ball fat and thin, as if the club had a mind of its own. I could only laugh and say "Oh really?!"

One last thing. If you are going to buy a "starter set," which is probably a good idea, please make sure that the club heads are stainless steel. I have seen many alloy club heads break because they were just plain cheap. If the word "stainless" is not printed on the club heads of a low priced set, ask if they are stainless, and avoid them if they are not. You can also assemble a starter set of your own. Good clubs to have are a Sand wedge, 9 Iron, 7 Iron, 5 Iron, 3 Wood, and Putter.

IMPORTANT TERMS

Before we move on to the good stuff, there are some terms with which you should be familiar so that we speak the same language. Everything is explained for a right-handed player. Just reverse the rights and lefts if you are left-handed. These are not in alphabetical order, they're more in golf order.

These are terms you need to know now, to help you learn. They will be used throughout the book.

Target line. A straight line drawn from the ball to the target.

Square. Aiming at the target (as in square club face) or parallel to the target line (as in square stance).

Club face angle. The direction in which a perpendicular line from the center of the club face points. Can be either **square** (line points to the target), **open** (line points to the right), or **closed** (line points to the left).

Club path. The direction in which you swing the club through impact. Can be either **inside-out**, or **outside-in** for the full swing.

Inside-out. The club head traveling in an arc from the left of the target line, out to the right as it approaches the ball. Stand behind the ball and imagine the target line (the line running from the ball to the target). To the left of the target line is inside. To the right is outside. **Inside-out** is how you are designed to swing and how the golf club is designed to be swung.

Outside-in. The club traveling from the right of the target line, across and to the left of it through impact. Known as a **pull**, this is the path which results in the dreaded slice.

> **CLUB PATH AND CLUB FACE ANGLE ARE THE TWO MAJOR FACTORS THAT INFLUENCE THE FLIGHT OF THE BALL.**

Stance line. A straight line drawn across the tips of your toes. Can be either **square** (parallel to the target line), **open** (to the right of the target line), or **closed** (to the left of the target line).

Shoulder line. The line across the front of your shoulders.

Address position. How you stand over the ball. Includes your posture, alignment and ball location.

Ball location. Where the ball is in your stance, relative to your feet.

Aim. Where the club face is aimed. See club face angle.

Alignment. Where *you* are aimed. You are aligned to the target when your stance line, shoulders, hips, and forearms are all parallel to the target line.

Club. The instrument used to send the ball to the target. An engineering marvel. That the club can be used to send so small an object so far with such accuracy (if used properly) is quite amazing, isn't it?

Club head. The whole thing at the end of the long skinny tube called a **shaft**.

Grip. The rubber part of the club that you hold.

Hold. How you place your hands on the grip.

Club face. The relatively flat, "front" of the thing at the end of the shaft that's designed to hit the ball.

Hosel. The part of the club head where the shaft is inserted.

Heel. The end of the club head nearest to the hosel.

Toe. The other end.

Iron. The sharp-edged, metal-headed clubs in a set.

Wedges. The most lofted irons in a set. Designed for hitting short shots that stop quickly. There are four types of wedges. In order from most to least lofted: Lob, Sand, Gap, and Pitching. The pitching wedge used to be used to hit pitch shots, hence the name, but since Gene Sarazen invented it in the 1930"s, the sand wedge has come along to take the pitching wedge's job. For the sake of clarity, it would be very helpful if golf manufacturers would call the pitching wedge a #10 iron and rename the sandwedge the pitching wedge.

Wood. Seldom made of wood anymore. These are large-headed clubs made for hitting your longest shots.

Driver. The longest of the woods. Use it to tee off on long holes.

Fairway wood. There are several, from a #3 to a #15. You'll probably find a set that comes with a driver, #3 wood and #5 wood. The #3 wood works great as a driver. A fairway wood with a number higher than #5 is considered a **utility wood**.

Pull. A ball that starts left of the target.

Push. A ball that starts right of the target.

Slice. A ball that makes a big curve to the right.

Fade. A small slice.

Hook. A ball that makes a big curve to the left.

Draw. A small hook.

Pull-hook. A ball that starts left and hooks.

Pull-slice. A ball that starts left and slices.

Push-hook. A ball that starts right of the target and hooks.

Push-slice. A ball that starts right of the target and slices.

Thin shot, aka skinny. Hitting just a little too high on the ball, making it fly lower than normal. Thin shots can turn out very well. That's called "thin to win," although your hands may sting a little.

Fat shot, aka chunky. Hitting the big ball (Earth) before you hit the ball. When you hit behind the ball, you have hit a **fat** shot. Also referred to as "heavy."

Topped shot, aka worm burner. Hitting the top of the ball, causing it to roll along the ground.

Shank. Hitting the ball with the hosel instead of the club face. The ball goes dead right. The only response is to say "Shank you very much."

The rest of these terms will clue you in about golf course talk.

Tee, aka peg. A little wooden stick that looks like a nail, on which you place your ball before hitting a **tee shot** (first shot on a hole) from the **tee box**. Put your ball on the tee first, before trying to push the tee into the ground.

Tee box. Usually defined by different colored markers between which you should tee your ball. Depending on how long you want the course to play, you can choose to play from any set of tees. The red tees are usually most forward (shortest). The whites are usually in the middle. And the blues are back farthest from the hole.

Par. The score an *expert* player would be expected to make on a hole. Not yet being an expert, you may want to make up your own definition of par, and evaluate your game by that. There are par 3's, par 4's, and par 5's, and you could be par for the course, or so many over or under par.

Bogey. One stroke more than par.

Birdie. One stroke less than par.

Eagle. Two strokes less than par.

Range. The driving range. Better said, the practice field. Where you learn the **mechanics** of the golf swing and ball flight control to prepare to play golf. Prepare is a much better word than practice.

Golf course. Where you play/learn **golf**. Definitely *not* where you learn or practice mechanics.

Practice green. Where you experiment to find out how to best get the ball into the hole. Ask someone in the pro shop if you are allowed to chip or pitch onto the practice green before you do.

Putting green. Where you do your best to get the ball into the hole. Please be careful when walking on this most delicate of golfing grounds.

Fringe, aka apron. A (twelve to twenty-four inch wide) strip of approximately 3/4 inch-high grass that surrounds the putting green. It separates the green from the rough and the fairway.

Fairway. The short grass between the tee box and the green. Try to hit it.

Rough. The high grass surrounding the fairway and the green.

Divot. The piece of ground dug up (sometimes) when you hit the ball. Always replace it so that it can grow back and so that golfers behind you don't have to hit their shot out of your divot (the rules say you can't move the ball out of a divot, and it really stinks to find your ball in a divot after you've hit a good shot into the fairway).

Ball mark. The indentation in the putting green made when the ball hits it. Fix it by using a tool made for the purpose, or by using a tee to pull the ground back into place. Tap the mark with the sole of your putter to smooth it out.

Green in regulation. The expert golfer is expected to be on the green of a par 3 in one shot, two shots on a par 4, and three shots on a par 5.

Bunker, aka trap. A hollowed out area of ground usually filled with sand, but sometimes just rough. Sand bunkers are more common than grass.

Hazard. Water and sand. Specific rules apply as to proper procedure. Please consult a rules book. Red or yellow stakes define water hazards.

Out of bounds, aka OB. Off the golf course. Defined by white stakes. Don't go here. If you do, the rules say you must add a penalty stroke and replay the shot from the same spot (called a stroke and distance penalty).

Through the green. The entire golf hole you are currently playing, from tee to green. Not, as it is mistakenly referred to, a ball that goes over or past the putting green.

SECTION 1

THE SHORT GAME

Listen. The short game accounts for about 67% of your score. If you want to improve your scoring, the short game is the place to start. By improving your putting only two strokes per round, you will instantly drop two strokes from your handicap. Hitting your drive twenty yards farther, even if it's straighter, won't do that for you. With that said, it is a sad but true fact that golfers rarely practice their short game. Maybe it's just more fun to bash the driver all over the range, but that's not golf. The only true measure of a golfer is score, and the fastest way to lower scores is a better short game.

This section will teach you everything you need to know about the techniques involved with putting, chipping, and pitching, including drills to help you learn the techniques and then put them to use. Be careful and teach yourself well, because while you are learning the short game, you will also be laying the foundation of your full swing.

1
PUTTING

Let's get right down to business. I have chosen to cover putting (and the rest of the short game) first, because I want to impress upon you the importance of learning to score. Putting can make or break you. You can save a lot of strokes over the course of a round if you are good with a putter. Likewise, you can ruin an otherwise good round with just a few bad putts.

Half of the strokes you use in a round of golf are with the putter, so you have to accept the fact that you will need to practice your putting (and the rest of the short game) at least as much as you practice your full swing. Another good reason to start with putting is that it is the simplest motion in golf, and mastering the technique will help you learn the other techniques required by golf much faster. As well, you will be making putts immediately as you do the drills I give you, and hopefully you will begin to feel that golf is not so hard after all.

Although there have been great putters who use a lot of wrist and great putters who use no wrist, I teach putting without wrist action because it is a simpler, more controllable motion. You will be able to control both your distance and direction much more easily with a wristless stroke. With that said, it is entirely up to you to decide how you putt best. However you choose to swing the putter, the drills in this chapter will make you a better putter, so practice them religiously.

HOLDING THE PUTTER

The **grip** is a part of the club. You **hold** the club. That's why I call it the putting hold, rather than the putting grip. There are just two important notes on how to hold the putter, otherwise it is a matter of personal preference.

1. **Thumbs go straight down the top of the shaft.** Hold the putter with its sole flat on the ground. You will be looking down at what we will call the "top" of the shaft. Most putter grips have a flat side on top of the shaft. Your thumbs should point straight down the flat side. You can lock your fingers together or overlap them in any way that feels comfortable.

2. **Palms face each other.** Try to align the grip along the lifeline of both palms. Your palms should face each other so that the backs of your hands are parallel.

Here are some of the most common methods of holding a putter. Give each a shot and see which works best for you.

OVERLAP

The Overlap hold is commonly used for the full swing, but you can use it for putting as well. Overlap your right hand little finger atop your left index finger.

REVERSE OVERLAP

The Reverse Overlap is very popular with golfers of all levels. Different from the Overlap hold, in the Reverse Overlap the left index finger overlaps the right little finger. Feel free to overlap more of your right hand (above) if it feels more comfortable.

LEFT HAND LOW

The Left Hand Low hold is gaining popularity among golfers for the following reasons: your shoulders are more level to the ground, which makes your stroke more level; the back of your left wrist is flat at address, which is where it should remain throughout the stroke; and your right elbow is closer to your body, which encourages a pendulum-like stroke and eliminates excess hand motion. Give this hold a try, it works!

PALMS AWAY!

The club rests very much in the palm of my right hand so that I can hold the club very loosely (for better touch) yet still control the club. Keep in mind that, more than anything, your putting hold needs to be comfortable.

PARALLEL HANDS

The palms of my hands are very nearly parallel. The most important thing to remember is that whatever your wrists do, the club head will also do, so keep your wrist movement to a minimum.

PUTTING SETUP

I don't want this to sound overly simple but, well, it really is simple. All you have to do is set your body, particularly your shoulders, parallel to the target line, let your arms hang straight down from your shoulders, and bend from the hips into a comfortable position. Then place the ball two inches left of the center of your stance, and make sure your eyes are directly above the ball. Once you find your most comfortable posture that allows your eyes to be over the ball, you may find that you have to slide your hands down lower on your putter grip. You can also have it cut down to fit you. Fit the putter to your setup, not your setup to the putter. I find that almost all of my students need their putter cut down to fit them.

THE BALL DROP

You will putt more accurately if your eyes are over the target line. While set up to a ball, drop another ball from the bridge of your nose to check the position of your eyes. The ball you drop should land on top of the ball on the ground.

TOO FAR FROM THE BALL
Eyes inside the ball won't accurately see the line to the hole.

RIGHT ON THE MARK
Eyes over the ball see the line much more accurately.

POOR POSTURE
Compare my posture in the near right photo to the photo on the far right. Standing too straight will cause my stroke to travel in more of an arc as it moves back and forward, rather than in a straight line, which can make consistency a problem. As well, my eyes are not over the ball.

GOOD POSTURE
My hands are directly below my shoulders. I'm comfortably bent over, yet enough to encourage a straight back and forward stroke.

A great way to get into the proper position is to hold the club in your right hand and let your left arm hang down natually. Then, without moving your left arm, use your right hand to place the club into your left.

THE IRON TRIANGLE

The **Iron Triangle** is one of the most important concepts you will learn from this book. It is the foundation of your entire golf game. You will use the Iron Triangle in every shot you play. This concept, once mastered, will help you gain accuracy in the short game, and both power and accuracy in the long game.

Put a club down on the ground and align your **stance line** (the line across the tips of your toes) parallel to the club shaft. Stand with your feet about six inches apart, legs slightly flexed. You will not have a club in your hands yet.

Now bend from the waist a comfortable amount and let your arms hang freely, straight down to the ground. If your hands are touching your legs, you need to bend more from the waist. Straighten your arms and press the palms of your hands together. Your arms form the **Iron Triangle**, which I will often refer to as the **Triangle**.

Now simply move your Triangle slowly back and forth without bending your elbows or wrists. Watch your hands and arms while you swing back and forth. Notice how your shoulders will have to control the movement in order to keep your Triangle intact.

Watch how your hands move while you move your Triangle. Notice that if you stand more erect, your hands move in an arc, and that as you bend over more, your hands move in a straighter line. Try bending over from the waist more or less to find the right amount of bend which allows you to effortlessly move your hands in a straight line back and forth.

- Make sure that you do not bend your arms or wrists, and try to keep your knees as still as possible.

- Feel that your shoulders are rocking up and down like a seesaw to move the Triangle.

The manner in which you are standing is called your **putting posture**, and I've been a little vague on purpose. I want you to assume a posture which feels comfortable to *you*. Some people will bend more than others, and some will stand very straight. There is no *right* way to do it, and that's just fine.

THE IRON TRIANGLE PUTT

Holding the putter as shown before, straighten your arms to form the **Iron Triangle**. Without hitting a ball, swing your Triangle back and forth in a pendulum-like motion. For starters, I'd like the length of swing to be about a foot back from, and forward of, your starting (**address**) position.

As you swing, watch your hands and arms, *not your putter*. You are trying to keep your arms and wrists from bending at all. Keep your knees, legs and hips as still as possible. **Do not hit a ball yet, just make certain that your technique is correct!**

The Iron Triangle provides a very concrete image that will apply to every golf stroke you ever make. With that said, it does not mean your arms should be rigid at all. Just maintain the triangle shape throughout the stroke.

Remember. The Iron Triangle is the foundation for your entire golf game. Every shot you ever make will require it. Learn it well.

THE IRON TRIANGLE

No breakdown in the wrists or elbows throughout the motion. Basically, the only moving parts are your hands, arms, and shoulders. Before you try this with a ball, make several swings watching your Triangle move. Keep it intact as you push back and forward. Also monitor your legs. Make sure that they remain very still as you swing.

DRILL

THE PUSH

Many beginning and intermediate golfers suffer through putting problems that stem from using a backswing that is too long for the length of the putt. The result is an inevitable deceleration through impact. All distance control is lost with such a stroke. The Push drill will help you avoid this problem.

SETUP

- Set your feet a comfortable distance apart.

- Position the ball two inches left of the center of your stance.

- Place your putter head directly behind the ball.

- Position your hands slightly in front of the putter head.

THE DRILL

Without any wrist action, push the ball into the hole, keeping your Triangle intact and the putter face aimed toward the hole all the while. Hold your finish and check to see that you did not break your Triangle, nor change the putter face aim. Fix your finish if need be. That will help you learn faster.

LESS IS BETTER

Some people prefer to have their arms and wrists bent at address for putting. If doing so feels more comfortable to you, feel free to. The important thing is that you do not change the amount of bend during the stroke. Extra movement can cause inconsistency in both putter face alignment and distance control.

DRILL

THE PUTTING TRACK

Lay down two clubs (2x4's work great, too) parallel to each other. Leave enough room between them to fit your putter head with one-half inch extra room on both sides. The shafts create a putting track that will help you learn to make a **square** stroke; back and forward along the target line. Center a ball between the clubs, and push the ball again.

Once it becomes easy to push the ball through the track without hitting either side, begin using a short backswing and forward push to stroke putts. Begin with a backswing of about four inches with an equal length or slightly longer follow through. If you find this drill very difficult, that means you are not ready for the ball yet. Just practice your stroke without the distraction of the golf ball until you own your stroke.

Be sure to watch the ball, not the putter, as you putt.

Don't bother to look at where the ball goes when you hit it. You are working on your stroke at this time, not trying to get the ball into the hole. If fact, you shouldn't be near a hole when you do this drill. It is vital that you have no target in mind when practicing your mechanics. Remember that!

As you get more proficient with the track drill, place the shafts (or 2x4's) closer together. If you can get them to a tolerance of one-eighth of an inch, you are just plain awesome.

ON TRACK

The benefit of a straight back and forward putting stroke is that there is much less chance for timing errors. If the putter is always square to the target line, you can't miss. No, it is not necessary that you have a perfect stroke, but it sure can't hurt.

MORE ON PUTTING

ABOUT DISTANCE CONTROL

You can go a long way toward improving your distance control by using only the Triangle to power the stroke. That way, you can control how far you hit the ball simply by adjusting the length of backswing you take—only one variable. If you use your wrists or elbows or, worse yet, body rotation to power the stroke, you force yourself to deal with many variables to send the ball the correct distance. That's not good science. Your forward swing will be slightly longer than your backswing as you accelerate through impact without becoming jerky or wristy. Keep your stroke smooth and rhythmic, and you will be well on your way to great putting.

Note: Many expert golfers lift the putter ever so slightly above the ground before they start the stroke. This is a great idea, as it prevents your putter from snagging in the grass on the way back and disrupting your stroke.

HOW SWEET IT IS

There is another factor that influences the direction and distance of your putts. You already know that the putter face must be aimed square to your target at impact for the ball to go there; that your stroke should be quite straight back and forward; and that you will control your distance by using shorter or longer strokes. However, you must also contact the ball on the sweetspot of the putter, otherwise, the putter will twist at impact, sending the ball off line and shorter than it would otherwise have gone.

To check where your putter's sweetspot is, hold the club up in one hand, and tap the face with the side of a coin until you find the spot where the club does not twist when you tap it. That's the sweetspot. It's not very big, is it? Using a magic marker, mark the top of the putter, even with the sweetspot, so that when you look down at the putter at address, the sweetspot's location is in clear view. Try to hit the ball with the sweetspot. Place some kind of tape or baby powder on the face so that impact will leave an impression, and you will know for certain whether you are hitting the sweet spot.

When you putt for real, make sure you do not work on your stroke. You must turn off your mechanical mind and focus on the target. You'll hear that again, because it is essential to playing good golf.

TARGET LOCK

As you take your last look at the target, say and do the "Target Lock." The idea is to lock the target in mind with your last look, slowly move your eyes back to the ball, and then start the motion while still seeing the target in your mind's eye. I have my students say "Target Lock" out loud just to remind themselves to do it. Lock onto a very small target like a blade of grass on the putting green, or a small spot in the fairway to allow your mind focus with precision. Target Lock every shot you hit. It pays off.

THE GRIND

Let me tell you about something I call The Grind. The Grind refers to the break-in period all golfers have to go through in order to *correctly* learn the skills required to play good golf. It takes strong commitment and perseverance to get through this period, and I am sad to say that many golfers never do make it. They expect golf to come naturally and it just doesn't. Whether you are working on your putting touch or your full swing, you will have to grind for a while. Make sure that you practice correctly so that you learn what you intend to learn. Grinding pays off, but only when you are ready. And you are not ready until you *own* your new skills. Don't give up. You weren't very good at tying your shoes when you first learned how, were you?

As you continue learning with this book, you are going to get a lot of mechanical ideas running through your head. Let me tell you, it's *hard* to let go of those mechanical thoughts and just concentrate on the target. Your ability to focus on the target will constantly be put to the test in golf. You are going have to practice that skill, just like you practice any other part of your game. It is precisely this sort of practice that enables good players to bring to the course, the same game they had on the range.

WATCH OUT FOR THESE MISTAKES

WRIST BREAKDOWN
You'll lose distance control and make it unnecessarily difficult to keep your putter face aimed at the hole during your stroke.

BODY ROTATION
You need to keep your legs and hips very still during your putting stroke, otherwise you will force the stroke off line.

STOPPING AT IMPACT
Your followthrough should be longer than your backswing. Take only as much backswing as you need, and accelerate through the ball, to the target.

Congratulations!

When you feel confident about the quality of your stroke, congratulate yourself on a job well done and realize that you are pretty much finished with the mechanics of putting. You should review your mechanics periodically, just to fine tune and maintain your good technique. But from now on, you should spend far more of your time doing the following drills, concentrating on the target only, without mechanics on your mind at all. Before you go on, however, you *really* need to know about the Pre-Shot Routine.

The Pre-Shot Routine, Part 1

Do you *really* want to get good? Then do this:

Before every putt, stand behind the ball, face the hole, and imagine the path the ball will take on its way into the hole. "See" the ball go into the hole, and "hear" the sound it will make as it clanks to a rest in the hole. Imagination is very important in golf.

Then take two or more rehearsal strokes while looking at the hole. *Rehearse* exactly what you intend to do (note: you may stand to the side of the ball rather than behind it, if it feels more comfortable). Don't practice your mechanics—you've already done that. Try to *feel* the stroke required to make the ball roll the proper distance. While you make these "feel it" rehearsal strokes, again imagine the ball rolling into the hole. You are creating a connection between yourself and the target, not practicing your stroke. The more clearly you can "see it" and "feel it," the better your connection will be. Get this point straight: Practice strokes are for working on your mechanics. Rehearsal strokes are for making putts.

While standing behind the ball, (you have not yet addressed the ball) pick out a small target, such as a blade of grass, that the ball will roll over (or toward) on its way to the hole, and lock that target in your mind. Try to see a path from your ball to the target.

Step up to the ball and **aim your putter**. Next, **align yourself** (take your stance) to the putter. Then run your eyes back and forth along the line to the target. Do this "tracking" with your eyes slowly, and try not to let your eyes "jump" along the line (that will take some practice). Then, when your brain tells you that you are ready, **putt the ball**. If it goes in, go take it out of the hole. If not, repeat the process.

This is only a small introduction to the Pre-Shot Routine, but it is absolutely imperative that you use your routine if you want to give yourself the best possible chance for success. You must have only the target in mind when you are practicing *making* putts. Technical thoughts will only interfere with your awareness of the target, and since the object is to get the ball to the target...

My routine

I don't think you should have the same pre-shot routine as anyone, but I want to tell you my routine so that you have a good idea of how to develop your own.

I start reading the green before I even step onto it. As I walk up to the green I notice the general lay of the land (sometimes it's difficult to get a clear idea of the severity of a green's slope when you're standing on it). I mark my ball and, without wasting much time at all, circle around the area of my putt to get a quick view from all sides. Then I squat down about ten feet behind the ball and try to visualize the way my putt will move as it rolls into the hole. I don't try to see a line, I try to see a path of balls stretching from my ball all the way to the hole. If, for instance, I determine that the putt breaks a foot right to left, I pick out a spot a foot to the right of the hole as my new target. If the putt is level, I move the spot a foot past the hole because I always want to give the putt enough speed to go in. If the putt is down hill, I move the spot closer. If it's uphill I move it farther away, but the direction remains the same.

Once I've got my new target, I forget all about the break. I'm now going to hit a straight putt to my *spot*—not the hole. This is when I'll make my rehearsal strokes. I prefer to make these while standing behind the ball, not to the side as you commonly see players do (I see better when facing the hole).

USE YOUR ROUTINE!

I'm not sure if "funny" is the right word, but it's funny how many times I have to remind students to go through their routine every time they have a target in mind. I guess some people feel like they're wasting valuable time on something unimportant. Listen to me now, and hear me later: You have to practice getting your brain in gear to hit your best shots, and it's too late if you wait 'till you get to the course to practice that.

Rhythm

I have an internal rhythm that feels comfortable to me, and I repeat this cadence, actually saying to myself, "one—two, one—two..." and make strokes to that cadence. I rehearse until I've got the right feel (don't limit yourself to a certain number of re-hearsal strokes), I then take my stance to the side of the ball and aim the putter.

Mini-routine

Before I stroke the putt, I have a short, mini-routine that I do exactly the same way every time. It's my start button, so to speak. While repeating my cadence, I take a last look at my spot, look back to the ball, and then go, all on the beat. It sounds like this: "One—two, one—two, look (to the target), look (back to the ball), back, through." It feels hurried at first, especially if you're used to freezing over the ball, but this way I am able to react to the target very much as Michael Jordan does when he shoots the basketball. He's not thinking, he's reacting to the target. Possibly the most important key to putting is a clear visual image of the target. Unfortunately, we don't get to look at the hole while we put, we are forced to hold the visual image in mind, which is much more difficult, but absolutely essential.

In sum, your Pre-Shot Routine should consist of three steps to program yourself for success:

1 **See it**. Visualize. See the shot as you want it to happen.

2 **Feel it**. Feel the amount of stroke, not the mechanics of the stroke.

3 **Do it**. Target Lock and go. Maintain your focus on the target you have in your mind's eye.

Following are several putting drills which you would do well to permanently include in your practice sessions. I realize that you probably have a job, maybe even kids, and that your time is limited, but if you skip putting practice, the score card will show it!

DRILL

AIMING EXERCISE

Aiming the putter face well is the most difficult part of making those short putts. This drill will show you exactly what a square putter face looks like and will train you to see the "line" to the hole. You can also use the tape to train your stroke.

On a level floor (short carpet works great) lay a piece of electrical tape in a straight line, fifteen feet long. The tape serves as your line to the hole. A great idea is to put a small mirror over the line at one end, just behind the ball, so that you can check that your eyes are over the line at address.

In address position, place your putter face perpendicular to the line and take a good look at it. That's what perfect alignment looks like. Moving only your head, look at the far end of the line, and then back to your putter face. Run your eyes back and forth along the line and absorb what perfect aim is. A well aimed putter may look strange at first. No problem. The more often you do this drill, the more familiar perfect alignment will look to you.

As a separate drill, make some strokes over the line. This will help train your stroke. And as another drill, try a few putts and see if you can keep the ball on the line. Start with short putts (two feet) and progress to the full length of the line. If the floor is not level, DO NOT PUTT ANY BALLS. You'll do more damage to your stroke than good.

AIM IS 90% OF PUTTING

Many golfers complain about pushing putts out to the right and pulling others to the left when, in fact, the problems stem directly from inability to accurately aim the club face. 90% of the club face angle error is transmitted to the ball's direction, while only 20% of the path error is. The point: Learn to aim your putter very well if you want to make putts.

DRILL

SHORT BUT SWEET

Find a straight, slightly uphill, one foot putt. It is most important to have a straight putt for this drill.

Place the ball one foot from the hole (target). Go through your pre-shot routine, and putt the ball. This drill will teach you to aim your putter face to the target, and to keep your putter head square to (facing) the target through impact.

Hold your followthrough and make sure that your putter face is still square.

After you get real good at this drill, increase the distance to two and then three feet. Twenty-five in a row from three feet is fantastic! For the really ambitious, try four and five footers, too.

I know one foot seems like an awfully short distance, but putting is all about confidence. You gain confidence by making lots of putts. You lose confidence by missing lots of putts. Don't practice missing. You might get good at it!

Another great drill is to practice putting to a small coin on the green (or the floor) as your target. Do this drill enough, and the hole will look like a basketball hoop.

ABOUT PRACTICING

It is very important to have a goal and a consequence in your practice. For example, having to start all over again can heighten your intensity, which will make your practice even more effective. Give yourself a specified amount of time to complete each drill and/or a certain number of putts you have to make, and force yourself to stay there until you reach your number, or run out of time.

READING GREENS

The science (art?) of green reading is learned through experience. It takes considerable time on the greens to learn how varying degrees of slope will affect the roll of the ball. To read a green properly, you must consider whether your putt will move uphill or downhill, break to the right or left, be into the grain or with the grain, or be affected by wind. Let me help you assess these variables.

To read putts, get at least ten feet behind the ball and squat down. You may want to walk to the opposite side of the hole and do the same thing. While you walk to the other side, keep looking around the hole. Circle around the hole to the other side as you return to your ball to get a view from all sides for the best read. As you walk around, be aware of your feet. They can help you feel the slope.

If, through surveying the area around your ball and the hole, you determine that the putt is downhill, meaning you are standing above the hole, you must keep in mind that the ball will roll farther than a flat putt. You will need to hit the putt more softly than a flat putt of the same distance. You may want to imagine that the hole is closer to you than it really is. In addition, since you are hitting the ball more softly, it will break (curve) more than a more level or uphill, breaking putt as it slows down. You will have to allow for more break on downhill putts.

When the ball is below the hole (you are putting uphill), you can afford to be more aggressive with your stroke. Definitely hit these putts hard enough to hit the back of the cup. Since you will hit the ball a little harder, it will stay on line better for you, so you can play a straighter line to the hole. Note that if you hit the ball too slowly on an uphill, breaking putt, the ball will break hard as it slows down. You may want to imagine that the hole is farther from you than it really is.

On breaking putts, you have to guess how much they will curve. Obviously, the more experience you have, the better your guess will be. After you determine how much the ball will curve, aim your putter not to the hole, but to a spot far enough to the side of the hole to allow the ball to break into the hole. For example, if I read six inches of break from left to right, I will pick a spot (a blade of grass for instance) six inches left of the hole and aim the putter there. I make that spot my target, and try to putt the ball there. This way, you can play all putts as straight putts. Be careful that your last look to the target is at your spot and not the hole. If you look to the hole, you'll putt the ball toward it rather than toward your spot. That's one big reason why average golfers fail to play enough break.

Most golfers, tour pros included, fail to play enough break when putting. Always give the ball a chance to roll into the "high side" of the hole and you will make more putts. (If the putt breaks right to left, the right side of the hole is the high side). A good idea is to double the amount of break you read, pick your spot, ignore the hole, and putt to your spot.

Southern golf courses usually have Bermuda grass on their greens during the warm months, and then overseed with another strain of grass such as Bluegrass for the winter months. Especially when playing on Bermuda greens, you must take note of what is called "grain." Grain refers to the direction in which the grass grows on the green. Grass grows toward water, or bends away from prevailing winds, and can significantly influence the roll of the ball.

Basically speaking, if the grass is shiny along the path to the hole, you are putting with the grain and the effect will be a faster putt. The opposite is true if the grass is dull, indicating that you are against the grain. When you are against the grain, the break will be more severe and the ball will stop sooner than normal. You need to hit putts firmly when putting against the grain. If you are putting a level putt, but the grain is going to the right, the putt will break right eventhough it looks dead straight. Grain will have some effect on all greens, although much more so on Bermuda, so take grain into account when reading all putts.

PRACTICE YOUR PUTTING

When most people practice, they completely ignore putting. They go straight to the range and hit drivers until they are too tired or frustrated to swing, and then they go home and sulk. Remember this. You can often make up for a poorly hit drive or approach shot, but when you miss a putt, the shot is lost forever. Include putting at every practice session if you want to shoot lower scores.

One more thing. Change the width of your stance to find out whether you putt better with your feet close or far apart. Do your drills with your feet close, and then do them again with them wider. A little experimentation could really make a difference!

DRILL

THREE BALL

For this distance control drill, take three balls and place them side by side, six inches apart, at a start distance of about fifteen feet from the hole.

Visualize the shot. Feel the right stroke: not how *to*, but how *much*. Step up to the ball. Aim your putter. Align yourself. Target Lock, and go. Don't hesitate and don't think. Just react to the target. Watch where the ball goes and adjust appropriately. If the last putt was too short, hit the next one farther, and vice versa. Go through your routine with each ball, and adjust each ball to the desired distance. If the last putt went in, do it again!

Do not evaluate how well you do this drill, there are no bad shots, only learning experiences. Simply let your mind soak up the information. Just think "that was neat, let's try this."

Do this drill from every distance you can find, uphill, downhill, and sidehill, and you will quickly improve your distance control. Try putting while looking at the hole and with your eyes closed to improve your ability to focus on the target throughout the stroke.

The idea of this drill is to give yourself more and more experience to rely upon for future putts. Read and stroke the first putt, then closely watch the ball roll to learn how accurate your read was. Then reread the next putt, now having a better idea of what the ball will do, thinking "so that's what that amount of break looks like." Do it once again for your third putt.

DISTANCE CONTROL

You definitely want to give yourself a chance to make the putt, but you don't want the ball cruising four or five feet past the hole. Attempt to get the ball just one foot past the hole, and you'll always be left with a tap-in, which is good for the blood pressure.

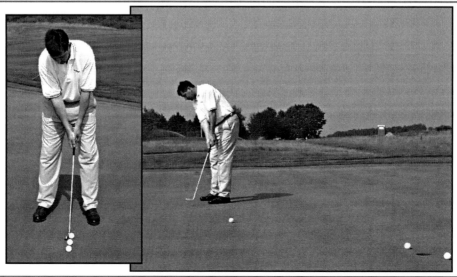

DRILL

THE LADDER

Starting fifteen feet from the target, place several balls in a straight line, three feet apart forming a ladder. Go through your pre-shot routine and start from the ball closest to the hole. **See it**, **Feel it**, and **Do it**. Then **Review it** if necessary. If the ball did not either go in, or about one foot past the hole, take a couple more practice strokes trying to feel the right one. Review strokes will help you learn just as much as your practice strokes and your actual putt.

Move on through all the balls with the same attention to your pre-shot routine, and please, for your sake, read every putt.

To make things a little more interesting, force yourself to get each ball within a three foot circle of the hole or start over again until you finish the whole ladder.

If there's enough room on the green, make sure your ladder reaches all the way to forty, fifty and even sixty feet. (The average birdie putt for the average golfer is forty feet.)

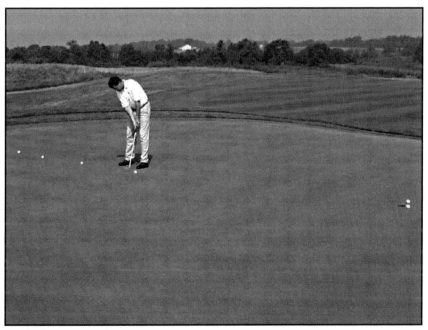

SPEED IS THE KEY

Distance putts are all about speed. How hard you hit the ball will not only affect how far the ball goes, it will also affect how much a putt will break.

DRILL

AROUND THE WORLD

By now, you are ready for an advanced putting drill which will help you with short, breaking putts. Place twelve balls in a circle around the hole, all two feet from the hole. Use a hole with some slope to it so that you can practice breaking putts. Go through your pre-shot routine (have you heard that before?), and putt the first ball. If you make it, take the ball out of the hole, put it aside, and go on to the next ball. If you miss it, replace it, and go on to the next ball. When you have gone through the circle of balls, go back to those you replaced and make five in a row from each spot. Around the World is a great short putting drill that will really help you lower your scores. Try to do it with three and four footers as well.

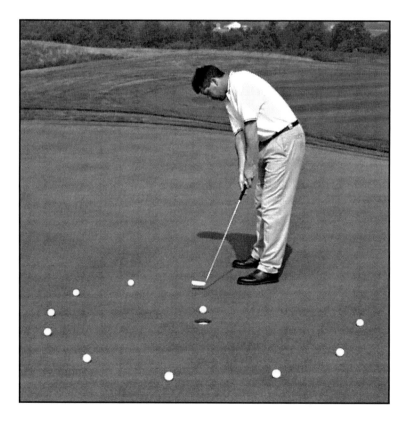

DRILL

FOUR CORNERS

Make four piles of five balls, and place them to the North, South, East, and West of the hole, three paces away (that's just about ten feet). Mark each spot with a tee or a coin. You must make three out of the five in order to go to the next pile. Again, you should use a hole with some break to it. Oh, make sure you use your routine. Have I said that enough yet?

Sometimes, these drills will take more time than you would really like. All I can say is, stick with them. They will lead directly to lower scores.

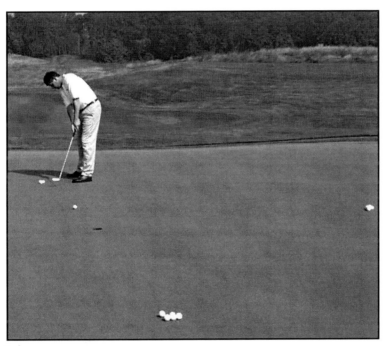

IT'S ALL CONFIDENCE

You can become a really good putter if you put in your time. Practice making lots of putts, and you'll think of yourself as a good putter. That's confidence.

DRILL

The Twenty Footer

Take three balls and place them seven paces from the hole (that's about twenty feet). Mark the spot with a tee. Take three more balls and place them on the opposite side of the hole at the same distance. Go through your routine each time, and try to putt the ball into the hole. If you get all three balls past the hole but within a putter's length of the hole, you get one point. Go to the other side and do the same. Your goal is to get to four points. The catch is that if any ball is not within a putter's length, you must start the drill over again from zero.

I'll tell you what, if you run through these drills every time you make it to the practice green, you can't help but get good. You can and will improve quickly if you put in the time and concentration. You just have to decide that you want to get good, and then commit to practicing regularly and for an extended period. Don't expect to be a scratch golfer after six months. That's crazy. You know what? Don't *expect* anything. Just practice because you enjoy it, and know you are on the path to good golf. You'll improve faster, having relieved yourself of the pressure your expectations put on you.

BETTER LONG THAN SHORT

Convince yourself to putt the ball past the hole, even if you are afraid of going too far. If you putt the ball three feet short, you will still be unsure of how the ball will break on your next putt. However, if you putt the ball three feet past the hole and watch carefully, you will know exactly how your next putt will break. That's the best read you can get! Also keep in mind that putts that don't reach the hole very rarely go in.

MAKE A GAME OF IT!

I certainly realize that the drills I have given you may make practice more like work. So here are a couple of games you can play with friends to make practice more fun *and* get a little pressure involved so you get used to making putts when it counts. My old friend, Mark (Clubber) Lange, who introduced me to the golf business, showed me these.

DRAW BACK

Draw back is a touch improving game in which the idea is to putt the ball to within one club length of the hole, but not short of the hole. If your ball ends up short of the hole, or more than one club length past or to the side of the hole, you must then draw the ball back an additional club length and then try to make it from there. Keep putting and drawing back as necessary until you get the ball into the hole.

These putts may be of any length. Practice relatively short putts (as close as 10 feet) as well as some long bombs and breaking putts. Play a specified amount of holes and keep track of total score. You will become a better putter under pressure *and* you'll enjoy your practice. You can't beat that with a stick!

21

With a friend, play closest to the hole from varying distances. You don't have to play the hole out. Here's how to keep score. Closest to the hole gets 1 point. Making the putt is worth 3 points. And if you make a putt after the other player has made it, you get 6 points and the other person gets 3. The first person to reach 21 points exactly, wins. You have to get 21 exactly. If you go over 21, then you go back to 15 and continue the game from there.

TWO PUTT

Play a specified number of holes (nine is good) and keep track of how many strokes you take for each hole. Par for each hole is 2, so you want to use 18 or fewer putts for the nine holes you play. One variation on this game is to continue playing sets of nine holes until you do use 18 or fewer putts. Another variation is to play the first nine, and then try to better your score on the second nine. If you don't better your score, you have to play nine more holes. A third variation is to play against someone else, and try to beat their score.

2
CHIPPING

We're going to move a little farther from the hole, to just off of the green. As we continue through the book, we will progress farther from the green until a full swing is required to get the ball to the hole.

The short game—putting, chipping and pitching—accounts for about 65% of the strokes all golfers use in a round of golf. **65%!!!** You owe it to yourself to have a really good short game. You may never hit a 300 yard drive like some of the tour pros, but you can have almost as good a short game. It's just a matter of a little technique and a lot of quality practice time.

Before we get into the actual chip, however, there are some things we have to get straight...

THE FULL SWING HOLD

I have included the full swing hold here because you must have it to chip the ball well. Although you can afford to be more of an individualist with the putting hold, as we move onto chipping, pitching, and the full swing, you will need a fundamentally sound hold that will help you deliver the club squarely to the ball, with the least amount of effort. A **square** club face aims straight to the target. If you hold the club improperly, you will have difficulty getting the club face square at impact. There are several points to learn about the hold, and they are all important. Practice your hold until it's automatic.

LEFT HAND

With your right hand, hold the club shaft (just below the grip) just about perpendicular to the ground. Your right hand should be chest high. The bottom (or leading) edge of the club face should point straight toward the sky. With the club like this, you will be looking at the "top" of the club. Visualizing a clock face, refer to the top as the "Twelve O'clock" position.

1. Move your left hand, fingers extended, to the side of the grip until you can put your fingers around it. When you take hold of the grip, your fingers should be just about perpendicular to the club shaft.

The club lay across the hand over these two points.

Thumb Pad

Heel Pad   Life Line

2. The heel pad, as opposed to the thumb pad, should rest on top of the club, lending support to your hold. Your little finger and ring finger will do most of the work holding the club.

3. You should see the first (big) knuckles of your index and middle fingers, possibly that of your ring finger too. The "V" formed by the index finger and thumb points to your right shoulder. Your left thumb should sit slightly to the right of the top, at the One O'clock position.

Heel Pad on Top

Be sure to look straight down when you check your knuckles. Don't tilt your head to the side. Your view won't be accurate.

RIGHT HAND

While holding the club in your left hand (with your new hold of course) here's how to place your right hand on the club.

1. Place your right hand so that the club rests mainly in the fingers. Although, in the end, all your fingers will be on the grip, your middle two fingers will do most of the holding.

2. The right side of your left thumb should rest in the life-line (the line between the heel pad and thumb pad) of your right hand. Your palms should face each other.

3. Your right thumb will sit slightly to the left of the top, at the 11 o'clock position; its "V" pointing to your right shoulder.

---

4. Use one of three ways to join your hands.

The Overlap	The Interlock	The Ten-finger
Place the little finger of your right hand over your left index finger, or between the index and middle fingers. This is the most common hold for men and stronger women.	Lock your hands together by inserting your right little finger between the left index and middle fingers. Use this hold if you have short fingers.	Bring your hands together so that the right little finger rests against the left index finger. This is a great hold for all beginners and children.

Here are a few checkpoints to remember about your hold:

- **Your hands should fit snugly together and share control over the club. Your palms should be parallel to each other.**

- **You will have two "V's" formed by the crease between the thumb and index finger of each hand. These V's should point to your right shoulder. You should see two or three knuckles of your left hand.**

- **Keep a constant eye on your hold. It will want to change on you at first, so make sure you review the keys.**

Now let's practice holding the club to ingrain the feel of the proper hold. Take your hands off the club and start all over again as before. When you are sitting in front of the TV, mindlessly watching something, practice holding the club. At least you'll be less likely to become hypnotized. When that becomes easy, and feels comfortable, rest the club head on the ground in front of you, and practice your hold.

Don't take your hold lightly (like that pun?). The hold is the first fundamental of golf. Before you ever attempt to swing the club, be automatic with your hold.

A COUPLE OF NOT-SO-HOT HOLDS

WEAK

My left thumb is directly on top of the grip, and my right hand is too far over to my left. This is an "open face" hold, and will cause the ball to curve to the right.

STRONG

My V's are over to far, pointing outside my right shoulder, and I can see four knuckles of my left hand. This is a "closed face" hold, and will cause the ball to curve to the left.

CHIPPING SETUP

A chip is a lot like a putt with a hop in it. The setup is the only major difference, and it will take just a little time to get comfortable with. Use a sand wedge or pitching wedge at first, then try using other clubs.

Stand with your toes about eight to ten inches from the ball, and position yourself so that the ball is even with the outside of your right heel. This may seem uncomfortably close at first, but trust me, it will become natural with a little practice. Your feet should be quite close together, about two or three inches between your heels is good. Shift your weight so that it is mainly on your left foot, but not so much that you are off-balance. Try to get your shoulders parallel to the ground.

To help you swing the club along the target line, your stance line should be slightly to the left of the target line. This is called an **open stance**, as opposed to a **square** (parallel to the target line) **stance**.

Now place your club right behind the ball, resting lightly on the ground. Don't push the club down into the ground because you may make the ball move, which is a penalty. Many good players hold the club slightly above the ground to avoid snagging the club in the grass on the backswing.

With your stance line left and your weight left, point your club shaft as nearly perpendicular to the ground as possible without forcing your hold to change. Push your hands forward, toward the target, until they are ahead of (closer to the target than) the ball and the back of your left wrist is flat. This **forward press** will set your hands exactly where you'll want them to be at impact. Be careful that you don't let the club face turn as you push your hands forward. With your setup complete, *get the ball out of the way before you attempt to learn the stroke!*.

Recall your **Iron Triangle** putting stroke. Without breaking your wrists or elbows, bring your Triangle back and then forward, as straight along the target line possible. To help learn the idea of a straight back and forward swing, you may want to practice your chipping stroke in the same manner as the Putting Track drill, (two clubs on the ground side by side). By the way, the chip and the putt are the only shots that use a straight back and forward stroke.

For now, forget about any target at all. Forget about the ball even. You need to be free to concentrate solely on your technique. Get the technique down first, and introduce the ball only after you are satisfied with your stroke. Then work on contact and accuracy using your good technique. It takes very little time to learn correctly the first time, but far longer to correct a bad habit.

CHIPPING KEYS:

The setup is very important. A good setup makes it easier to contact the ball solidly. That's the reason for such a detailed description. It may seem a little uncomfortable, but it works.

1. **Stand about eight to ten inches from the ball and position the ball even with the outside of your right heel.**

2. **Align your stance slightly left of the target.**

3. **Put your weight on your left foot.**

4. **Push your hands forward, ahead of the ball until the back of your left wrist is flat.**

5. **Swing the Iron Triangle back and through (your backswing should be slightly longer than the forward swing).**

SETUP FOR SUCCESS

Weight left, stance aligned left, hands well in front of the ball. The set up may feel strange at first, but it makes solid contact much easier to achieve.

DRILL

THE IRON TRIANGLE CHIP

Setup as described. Take note of the position of your hands and wrists at address. Make an **Iron Triangle** backswing of about eighteen inches from the ball and stop. Check to see if your wrists have bent. If they have, start again. Try to remove as much wrist action as possible, but avoid being rigid, or "death gripping" the club. A little looseness in your hands is good for touch. Be particularly aware of your left wrist. It will try to bend on you, and that will ruin your chipping, not to mention your entire game.

Now swing forward through impact, pushing the club both down toward the target and forward toward the target at the same time. Hold your finish position and check your wrists and arms. *NO BENDING!!!* Make sure that you check both backswing and followthrough. Don't break the Iron Triangle!

DRILL

THE LONG CLUB

The Long Club is a tool I use to help my students learn the proper chipping technique. It works magic for students who errantly break their wrists during the stroke. I have cut a hole in the butt of the grip on my wedge and inserted an old shaft so that about two or three feet of the old shaft protrudes from the butt of the wedge. Take your normal hold on the wedge, and let the extra length of shaft rest against your body, under your left arm. Don't rest the shaft against your arm, It should touch your body just above your belt.

Practice chipping as usual, but don't let the shaft come off of your body at any time during the stroke. If you get wristy with your backswing, the shaft will leave your side.

THE IRON TRIANGLE: A GOLFER'S BEST FRIEND

Just as in putting, the Iron Triangle image will greatly help you learn. The Long Club makes it easy to learn the perfect motion. You can also use The Long Club for shorter pitch shots, covered in Chapter 3.

DRILL

DOWNWARD CONTACT

Keep in mind that you must try to hit the ball as your club is moving downward, toward the ground. A descending attack into impact will help you make solid contact. The loft of the club will get the ball in the air for you. On longer shots, the backspin created by hitting down the back of the ball will get the ball up. You need not ever help the ball up by lifting or scooping it. You may want to make several practice swings where you take your backswing and then push the club down into the grass until your club cuts through the grass and hits the ground. Remember The Push drill in the Chapter 1? This is the same push move, but on a different angle.

Setup as normal, but place another ball about eight inches behind the original ball. Chip the ball you've setup to, making sure you avoid the one behind. If you do not descend sharply enough, you'll hit the wrong ball. Instant feedback. I love that!

A LEANING CLUB SHAFT

Make sure you stop and hold your finish so that you can check this key position. To strike the ball solidly, your hands must be ahead of the ball at impact, creating a club shaft that leans forward.

Keeping your weight on your left foot throughout the chipping stroke will also help you make solid contact. Try lifting your right heel off the ground a couple of inches and keep it there through the shot. Your weight will have to stay left, just as it should.

DRILL

PICK A SPOT

After you get your technique down, it's time to move on and try to make your chips go in the hole. You should monitor your technique from time to time, but the point of learning the correct technique is to forget it and just hit the shot.

Get a small towel or handkerchief and place it on the ground or the putting green as a target. Using a sand wedge, try to chip balls onto your target. Get used to the idea of picking a spot onto which you will land your chips. You can do this drill at the putting green, or in the backyard. All that's left is to learn how far the ball will roll, and that's easy. Get to a putting green where they allow chipping, and hit lots of chips and watch what happens.

Soon you will need to get good at imagining how far you want the ball to fly and how much it will roll. As you take your practice swings, try to feel how big a stroke you need. Remember that the rehearsal strokes are for feel, not for mechanical correctness. Whenever there is a target, forget your mechanics and concentrate on the target.

Try different clubs with the same target. Watch the difference in the way the ball rolls as you change from club to club. You need to try a lot of shots, from as many different positions as you can think of, to give yourself as much experience as you can. Experience is the key. If you are trying a shot for the first time, you may not be very good at it. But if you've practiced it before, you'll have a much better chance of success.

FLAT LEFT WRIST

Notice how flat my left wrist is at the finish of this short chip shot. This is imperative for club face control and distance control, and it greatly improves the quality of contact.

DRILL

UP AND DOWN

This drill introduces the idea of scoring. The idea of the drill is to chip the ball UP, close to the hole, and then putt it DOWN, into the hole. Two shots is the goal, but if you need more, go ahead, don't give up. This drill is what golf is all about: getting the ball into the hole in the fewest strokes possible. Set a goal for yourself. Don't end the drill until you have made a certain number of up and downs. Start with five and then increase your goal as you improve.

Note: Generally speaking, I like to have my students first develop good touch with the sand wedge and 9 iron, and then introduce the other clubs later. For now, use the sand wedge (or pitching wedge, if that's what you have) for shorter shots (within about thirty feet of the hole), and 9 iron for longer shots. A good guideline to follow is to fly the sand wedge one half the distance to the hole, letting the ball roll the remainder of the distance. Fly the 9 iron about one third the distance to the hole. Land the ball on the green whenever possible—the ball will bounce straighter on the green.

As you advance, spend some time practicing with the sand wedge through the 6 iron. You may find it easier to control your distance simply by using the same stroke and letting the differently lofted clubs send the ball farther or shorter. The more lofted clubs will roll the least, which is good for short chips, and the less lofted ones will give you the most roll, which can be used for longer chips.

Congratulations!

Ok, if you can honestly say to yourself that your chipping technique is sound, and you don't have to think about it when you chip, congratulate yourself and realize that you are done with the mechanics of chipping. You may need to review the mechanics periodically, but it is time to leave technical thoughts behind. You can now trust your technique, and focus your attention on the target. Become target oriented, not mechanics oriented. That's how you *PLAY GOLF.*

WATCH OUT FOR THESE MISTAKES

WRIST BREAKDOWN

Just as in putting, if your wrists break through impact, you invite a host of problems. Your hands must be ahead of the club head at impact which will make the club shaft "lean" forward, ensuring downward contact. No bending either the wrists or elbows, please!

BALL LOCATION TOO FORWARD

Positioning the ball too far forward can make contact very difficult.

Remember. The ball is positioned even with the outside of your right heel. As you advance, moving the ball forward helps you hit higher, softer chips. Try that later.

3
PITCHING

Moving right along... A pitch is a longer, higher version of a chip. Pitching includes the wide range of distances which require a longer swing than a chip, but a shorter than full swing. Let's just say, for our purposes, that a chip becomes a pitch when you have to carry the ball five yards or more in the air. The neat thing is that the same drills you do to learn pitching will also help you learn the full swing. In fact, I nearly always use pitching to help illustrate key full swing concepts; because the swing is slower, students are more aware of the club in their hands. We will start with address position, and then move onto the drills. I have found my students' progress to be nothing short of amazing by using these drills, and I suggest that you start every practice session with them. Use a sand wedge, or pitching wedge if you haven't got a sand wedge. You *really need* a sand wedge, however.

By the way, considering the name, it would seem sensible to use the pitching wedge for pitch shots, but that is not so. The advent of the sand wedge came about late in the history of the game, well after the pitching wedge was around. It would be more accurate to think of the pitching wedge as a 10 iron, and the sand wedge as a pitching wedge for more clarity. The sand wedge is absolutely not limited to shots from the sand.

Address Position

Basically, address position refers to the way in which you stand to the ball. Address position is important because it *can* set you ready to make a good, balanced swing. Or not. Your posture, alignment, and ball location make up your address position.

Here are the keys:

- **Stand straight with your feet directly under your shoulders and hold the club straight out in front of you.**
  Note: How far apart you set your feet will vary with club selection and the type of shot you are going to hit. Generally, play all *full* shots with the ball within two inches of the inside of your left heel. More on ball location later.

- **Flex your knees until you feel your thigh muscles just begin to work.**
  You want to feel like you are solidly rooted to the ground, providing a strong base from which to make your swing.

- **Push your behind out just a little, in order to keep your back straight and tilt your spine forward from your hip joints until the club hits the ground.**
  This should feel similar to the start of sitting down.

- **Let your arms hang straight down from your shoulder sockets.**
  Hang loose! Tension kills golf swings.

- **Tilt your spine slightly to the right.**
  Because your right hand is lower on the club than your left, your right shoulder is also lower than your left. Therefore, your spine tilts slightly to the right. Allow this tilt to occur. Don't try to level out your shoulders. Just let them relax.

- **Place your hands slightly in front of the club head.**

- **Place your weight about 70% on your heels (you should be able to wiggle your toes comfortably), and 60% on your right foot.**

Now, check your balance and your tension level. You want to feel like you are set solidly into the ground like a tree. To check my students' address position, I will give them a little push backward and then forward. If they fall off-balance, we know they require a change in either knee bend or waist bend. Watch out for your weight getting too far out over your toes. That's probably the most common error, and it sets you off balance right from the start.

POSTURE CHECK
Bend your knees just enough to feel your thigh muscles engage and allow your arms to hang loosely from your shoulders. A line drawn from the middle of your shoulder should fall on top of your toes.

ALIGNMENT is another part of address that is crucial for successful shotmaking. There are four components of alignment which you must check every time you set up to the ball. Lines across your **feet**, **thighs**, **shoulders**, and **forearms** should all be parallel to the target line. Always practice with a club on the ground to serve as an alignment aid, and you will go a long way toward getting the most out of your practice.

SOLID ADDRESS
Perfect balance combined with feet, thighs, shoulders, and forearms aligned parallel to the target line. Note also that, from this view, the butt of my club points at my belt.

That was an awful lot of talk about the address position and it's important, but you need not ever think about it while swinging the club. Address position is a **pre-swing fundamental**. Once you set yourself properly, don't give it another thought. Obviously, setting yourself correctly will take time at first, but you will soon be able to do it without much thought at all. Keep in mind that when you address the ball, you can help yourself a lot by checking (and releasing) tension before you swing.

Ok. We will start pitching with a simple drill to teach you the real meaning of the "followthrough," called the **push**. Then we'll move onto an extension of the chipping motion called the **Iron Triangle Pitch,** and finish off the longer pitches with the **Three Quarter Pitch**. But first, an important note from the coach...

DO THESE DRILLS SLOWLY AND PERFECTLY!!!

Your improvement is directly related to the quality of your practice. Practice makes permanent. *Perfect* practice makes perfect. So practice perfectly and you will learn the right stuff. Fast. The following three drills should be done at the start of every practice session. As you first learn your swing, the drills will teach you the proper technique. They will also help you to maintain your swing throughout your career.

Listen. Eighty percent of the golfers in this country suffer from a disease called the slice. The slice is caused by a combination of the wrong **club path** and the wrong **club face angle**. Starting with this section, you will learn the proper mechanics (inside-out club path, and club face control) which will enable you to hit the ball with power and control if, and only if, you practice correctly. It is far more important to do fewer repetitions of *perfect* quality, than to do more repetitions of *almost* perfect quality. Impatience is your adversary. If you follow the instruction in this book, you will learn very quickly, but at your own pace. Be patient! Once again, DON'T INTRODUCE THE BALL UNTIL YOU ARE *VERY* COMFORTABLE WITH THE TECHNIQUE.

When you learn to ski, you don't jump on a double diamond run to start out, do you? The equivalent to doing that is to head to the golf course with a bunch of new ideas about how to swing the club, and try to practice your new moves during the round. Well, at least you can't get hurt on a golf course, but you won't learn anything either. If anything, you may *think* you are doing something different, but may actually be making the same old mistakes. The conclusion you'll invariably come to is that the new stuff doesn't work, although you never actually did it right in the first place.

The key is to practice in the backyard or at the range slowly and with complete conscious control, so that you learn exactly what you are trying to learn. There are a lot of golfers out there who have taken the right instruction, only to go out and teach themselves something different. I strongly advise against that. There are also lots of golfers who have been given the wrong instruction and learned it perfectly. Well, all I can say is that, at least, this *is* the right instruction. Now it's up to you to teach yourself well. You have to ingrain the feel of the correct mechanics before you can use those mechanics. When I see a new student for the first time, I tell him/her, "Up to this point you may not have known how to practice well. I promise to teach you exactly what to practice and how, so from this point forward, if you practice wrong, it's your own fault." I'm just the coach. *You* are the teacher. Teach yourself correctly.

DRILL

THE PUSH

This is going to seem a little too easy, but please do The Push at the start of each practice session. No ball, please. Use your long club if you've made one.

The whole drill goes like this: Start at address and swing forward to what I call the **followthrough**. Sounds simple, but you must learn to push the club toward the target without breaking your Triangle, *and* allow your hips to rotate at the same time. Although your Triangle will lead your hips just slightly, your movement should be smooth and seamless.

Let me make it clear that the "followthrough" is different from the "finish." The followthrough is extension toward the target and occurs throughout the downswing. The followthrough ends when: the club shaft is nearly parallel to the ground and pointing toward the target; the Iron Triangle is still intact (no bending at the elbows or wrists); your hands are in front of your belly button; your belly button points to the target or to the left of it (if you can turn that far); your left leg is straight, holding virtually all of your weight on it; and your right shoulder is lower than your left. The **finish** is the final resting place of the full swing, and we are not doing that just yet. You own this drill when you come to the perfect followthrough automatically.

PUSH THE CLUB TOWARD THE TARGET

Note the complete extension of my arms as they push the club toward the target. Also note the straight the line from the front of my chest down my left leg is (second photo). You want to push forward without leaning your upper body forward.

FOLLOWTHROUGH KEYS:

- **Belly button facing the target.**

- **Iron Triangle intact. Arms straight, wrists straight.**

- **Hands belly button high or higher, club shaft points to the target.**

- **Left leg straight with almost all of your weight on it.**

- **Right foot up on the toe, virtually weightless.**

- **Right shoulder lower than the left.**

I think I need to explain why you should be so picky about this drill. For maximum power, you need to accelerate the club head all the way through impact toward the target. In order to continue your acceleration through impact, your hips must rotate. If your hips don't rotate, you cannot possibly extend toward the target, and you will lose both power and control. If your wrists bend improperly, club face control becomes difficult, making consistency elusive. Your left leg supports your body weight on the down swing. It must straighten as it receives your weight, or you will find it difficult to turn forward completely or make solid contact consistently. Finally, your spine angle must remain quite constant through impact to make good contact consistently. That means that if you stay in your posture (maintain your spine angle) as you turn on the backswing, your left shoulder will automatically be lower than your right (we haven't done the backswing yet), and as you followthrough, your right shoulder will be lower.

SPINE ANGLE REMAINS THE SAME

Note how my spine angle has remained the same from address to the followthrough that's really important for making solid contact.

HIP ACTION

Train your body to properly rotate as the club pulls it around on the down swing with The Push.

FULL SWING ADDRESS AND PITCHING ADDRESS

The differences between the full swing and a pitch shot are address position and swing length. For a pitch, you will set your weight firmly on your left foot at address and keep it there throughout the shot, whereas in the drill, you start from full swing address. This also is true for the Three Quarter Pitch that follows.

Make certain that you understand the difference between **full swing address** (weight 60% on your right foot, right leg supports backswing), and **pitching address** (weight 90% on left foot, left leg supports entire swing).

FULL SWING ADDRESS   PITCHING ADDRESS

BALL LOCATION
Note the difference in ball location (where the ball is relative to my feet). For all full swings, the ball is within two inches of the left heel, but for all pitch shots, the ball is near the right foot. For short pitches, as in the Iron Triangle pitch, play the ball even with your right foot, as shown here. For longer pitches, move the ball just inside the right heel, as on page 81.

PITCHING ADDRESS
My shoulders are more level and my weight is firmly on my left foot, where it will stay throughout the swing. My feet are very close together. Ball location is back toward my right foot, and I stand closer to the ball than for a full swing.

FULL SWING ADDRESS
Stance line (line across toes) is **square** (parallel) to the target line.

PITCHING ADDRESS
Stance line is **open** (to the left of the target line).

GET THE SWING RIGHT FIRST!

Do not use a ball when you first do any of the drills I give you. Just watch yourself and get used to the motion. When the swing becomes easy to make, then add a ball.

When you add the ball, tee it up about one-half inch above the grass, or if on a mat, use the rubber tee provided. While you are learning your swing, you should absolutely, every time, tee the ball up to make contact as easy as possible. **You *must* understand that, at this time, you will focus on sending your energy, via the club head, to the target, not on contact.** Contact is so easy that you can actually hit the ball with your eyes closed (my students do this just to prove the point to themselves). You must learn to swing to the target, not at the ball, otherwise you will ruin your swing. Let the ball get in the way of a swing toward the target. This is one of the major reasons why golfers don't improve: They work on their swing, try to get the ball to a target and do everything in their power to make contact all at the same time. That's a sure formula for Attention Deficit Disorder, folks. You can't do it that way. Do not sacrifice your swing, or your awareness of the target, just to make contact. If you concentrate on the ball, the target disappears. If you concentrate on your mechanics, the target disappears. Golf is a target game. Imagine shooting darts without knowing where the dart board is. That's how most golfers play golf. No wonder the average golf score is 100!

When you are ready, introduce the ball. When things are going well with the ball teed up, put the ball on the ground and try hitting to a small target. Use your pitching address now. Use other balls out on the range as targets, and hit everything from short chips to thirty yard pitches and try to land the ball you are hitting on top of your target ball. For the most effective practice, go through your pre-shot routine (**See it**, **Feel it**, **Do it**), and switch targets each ball.

Also realize that you have to allow for the ball to roll after it hits, you don't want to fly the ball all the way to the hole. I know that's a little obvious, but I felt I should say it. The best way to get a feel for how much the ball will roll is to hit lots of pitches to a real green, and pay close attention to how the ball lands and rolls. You'll probably find it difficult to find a good practice green where pitching is allowed, so the next time you go to the course, you might want to ignore your score and hit a couple of extra pitches each hole. Just be careful not to do that when other golfers are waiting behind you, or you might find golf balls raining around you.

DRILL

THE IRON TRIANGLE PITCH

Pitching is all about distance control, not just raw distance. The amount of backswing you take will dictate how far the shot flies, and so I offer you two different backswing benchmarks over the next few pages to help you gain a good feel for pitches of varying lengths. Once you have the feel of these two backswings, it will be relatively easy to judge the shots in-between your benchmarks.

All golf shots require the fundamentals you will learn from the pitching. I often use pitching to help students learn the full swing because the pitch is so much slower and more controllable. So not only will you learn a short game technique that you must *own* if you want to play good golf, you will also build a rock solid foundation for your full swing. You see, there *is* a madness to my method!

Just so you know, this backswing should generate only twenty to twenty-five yard shots. It's not about how far you can hit the ball. You just want to know exactly how far the ball will fly in the air with this length backswing *every time*. You may want to start this drill using full swing address and then, when you are comfortable with the motion, change to pitching address.

THE IRON TRIANGLE PITCH (BACKSWING)

No wrist or elbow bend. Most golfers ruin their swing in the first two or three feet of movement. Take care to get this drill right and you'll make golf easier.

Start the backswing by moving your Triangle back until the club shaft is parallel to the ground, and no higher than your belt. This shot won't require any wrist or elbow bend, otherwise, you'll hit the ball farther than you expect. Then, smoothly accelerate the Triangle forward, through impact, until *your Triangle forces your hips to rotate* in order to continue the swing. Stop at the followthrough, as you learned in The Push. Your arms should be straight as a result of the pushing motion, but not tight, and your hands should be very loose.

When using full swing address to help build your full swing, maintain the flex in your right knee as you move the Triangle backward, so that you feel your weight shift onto your right leg. Note that you should not have to force the weight shift. The motion of your arms, hips and shoulders, combined with a firmly flexed right knee should make the weight shift automatic. When you change to pitching address for the actual pitch shot, keep your weight on your left foot throughout the motion.

Some movements that go on in your swing result from previous movement. The weight shift is one of them. Turn properly on the backswing, and your weight will shift, but don't *try* to shift your weight. When you push the club forward through impact, your weight will shift forward. While you move one part of your body, another part may move out of necessity. You must not try to avoid movement. Train yourself to move what has to be moved and allow other movements to occur naturally.

THE TRIANGLE PULLS THE BODY AROUND

The Iron Triangle pulls the body through impact and on to the followthrough. I'm extending my club, hands, and arms out to the target, just as though I were to toss a ball there underhanded.

THE THREE QUARTER BACKSWING

When it comes time to hit longer pitches, you will need to lengthen your backswing. **The Three Quarter Pitch** will give you a second benchmark distance, to which you can add or subtract as needed. Say your Three Quarter Pitch carries the ball fifty yards and you have thirty-five yards to your target. You know that the correct length backswing is somewhere between Iron Triangle and Three Quarter, so you can make a very educated guess as to the right length backswing.

Mechanically speaking, many people ruin their golf swing before they ever get near impact. They have difficulty extending and properly setting their wrists on the backswing. This drill, done slowly and accurately, really speeds the learning of one of the most complex motions in the golf swing. Once again, not only do you learn a vital short game skill, but you work on your swing at the same time. I love this job!

Ok, here we go. Let's do this from **full swing address** first, then turn it into a pitch shot.

Take your Iron Triangle backswing and stop. Then, use your right hand to point the club up to the sky. That's called the **wrist set** (or wrist cock). The butt of the club should point at the target line if you're looking in a mirror, or at the ball, if you're turning your head and checking your position. As your right hand points the club up, your right elbow will bend in reaction. **Remember. Your right elbow bends as a reaction to your wrist set**. It should not bend before you set your wrists. As your right hand points the club up, push your left hand back away from you. Feel as though you are keeping your left hand as far away from your body as you can. This pushing back will cause your shoulders to continue turning as you make your backswing. As well, it will widen the arc of your swing, giving you more power. Be sure to brace your right leg and maintain the flex you set in your right knee at address, so that **your backswing will cause your weight to shift to your right leg**.

The Three Quarter backswing is complete when your left arm is parallel to the ground, the club shaft and left arm form a ninety degree angle, the butt of the club points at the target line and your hands are in front of your right biceps muscle.

> You already know that the target line extends from the ball to the target, but it will help to imagine that the target line extends out past the target and back behind the ball.

BALL LOCATION

Note the difference in ball location between the chip, pitching address, and the Three Quarter Pitch. The chip has the ball behind the right foot. Play short pitches with the ball even with the right foot. The Three Quarter Pitch has the ball just inside the right foot.

Once you complete the backswing, you have only to push the club head forward to the followthrough. But before we go further, I want to make this down swing business a little clearer. The next two pages are really important.

> Your hands and arms cause the down swing. Your right arm extends back and down while your hands swing the club head by pushing against the club shaft. As you continue pushing back and down, the motion turns into forward, on through impact, toward the target. Your hands and arms will pull your body around behind them.

The **transition** (the move at the top of the backswing that causes the down swing) is where my instruction really breaks tradition. There seems to be a near conspiracy against golfers, designed to keep them in need of a lifetime of lessons and the latest magic clubs. Some of the instruction that we consider classic has made it all but impossible for the average golfer to swing the club toward the target. As I've said, eighty percent of all golfers slice the ball, largely because they do what they've been told. It's as simple as this: The best way to swing the club toward the target is to extend back and down first. Any other movement will cause the club to move off-line, requiring a mid-swing compensation the average golfer simply can't make.

DRILL

THE THREE QUARTER PITCH

MAINTAIN A WIDE ARC

Notice the distance between my hands and my chest. Left arm parallel to the ground. Ninety degree angle between club shaft and left arm. Hands in front of right biceps. Also notice the club shaft angle in the photo below. The angle will change as I start the down swing.

THE TRANSITION

Hands and arms start the club head *back* and *down* before my shoulders or hips turn forward. The club head is *behind* me. Note the directions: OUT (right) is the most common mistake in golf; DOWN (to the ground); BEHIND (left); FORWARD is toward the target. BACK is opposite the target. Note the difference in the club shaft angle from the previous photo. It has "flattened" (become more horizontal).

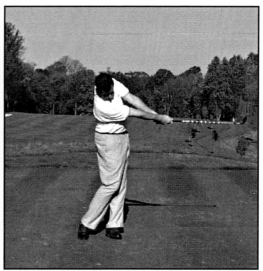

IMPACT

I am still pushing the club down through impact and my hips are responding to the pull of my arms by rotating in a tight pivot. The club shaft is leaning forward toward the target slightly ensuring that the club head will hit the ball first and then the ground. It helps to feel that you are trying to push the club head down even after impact, and keep it low even after the ball is gone.

THE FOLLOWTHROUGH

At this point, the Triangle is still intact, as I have extended my energy toward the target. It's a powerful move through the ball that you'll see in all good golfers. I have not forced my weight to shift forward, it has happened naturally.

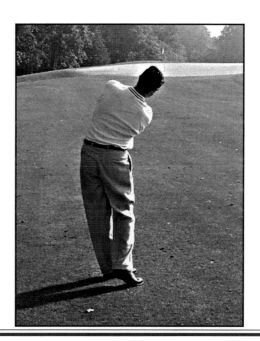

KEYS TO THE THREE QUARTER PITCH

BACKSWING

1. Your right hand sets your wrists and your left hand pushes back away from you, as you bring your hands up, even with your right biceps muscle.

2. The butt of the club points at an extension of the target line.

3. Your left arm and club shaft form a right angle.

4. Your right knee has firmly maintained its flex, allowing your weight to shift to your right leg.

DOWNSWING

1. Extend your right arm back and down while you swing the club head with your hands. Just after you start the downswing, the club head should move behind your back as the club shaft tilts flatter (more parallel to the ground) than at the top.

2. Your body does not turn forward until you feel your hands, arms, and the club head pull it around.

3. The club shaft leans slightly forward at impact (hands ahead of club head). One of my favorite swing keys is "thumbs down through impact," meaning push your thumbs down toward the ground and keep them pointing downward for as long as you can through impact and even into the followthrough.

4. Stop at the followthrough. Check hips, Triangle, left leg, weight, and right shoulder.

Your right hand will push against the club shaft continuously throughout the down-swing to accelerate the club head down through impact. Your right forearm will also thrust the club head into and through impact. Your right hand and forearm are the two major power sources in your swing. Your body's forward rotation, while necessary, is only a minor source.

Your left hand will guide and control the club face. It adds some speed to the swing, but your right hand and arm are the main accelerators.

MAKE YOUR PRACTICE COUNT

Golfers often have the best intentions when they practice, but still don't improve nearly as fast as they could. Some even get worse. *How* you practice is extremely important. You are a perfect learner. You are going to learn whatever you practice, so practice perfectly. I describe two types of practice to my students: **Precision Practice** and **Haphazard Practice**.

Precision practice requires discipline. You have to make sure you practice correctly. Don't trust your feel. What you *feel* is not necessarily what you *do*. You must have some sort of objective and accurate feedback if you want to practice precisely. Video-tape yourself. Get in front of a mirror. Or have a friend who knows what's right help you. Rush through the movements without total awareness or accurate feedback, and you practice haphazardly. That's a good formula for learning bad habits. That's why so many golfers fail to improve.

Obviously, you know how I want you to practice, but you will have to keep a constant eye on yourself to make sure you *always* practice precisely. Before every swing, ask yourself, "What *am* I doing out here?" Whether you are working on mechanics, or getting the ball to a target, know what you are working on, and concentrate only on that. Don't waste your time. Chances are, you don't have much of it. You can learn the golf swing really quickly if you want to. It's all in the quality of your practice. The following is exactly how I want you to practice.

START WITHOUT A BALL! You've got to be tired of hearing that by now, but are you doing it??? Make your Three Quarter backswing and hold it. Look. Check for accuracy. Make sure it's right. When you take a look back, make sure you stay in your posture. Don't stand up straight. Then watch the club as you start the downswing. The **club shaft** should flatten and the **club head** should move *behind* you as your hands push and your right arm extends to move the club *back* and *down*. Then allow your hips to be pulled around as you continue pushing and extending toward the target. Stop at the followthrough, and check again.

It is a great help to think that you will always use the Iron Triangle Pitch move through impact. Look at it this way: On the backswing, you start with the Iron Triangle backswing; continue on up to the Three Quarter backswing; move **back down** to the Iron Triangle backswing; and do the Iron Triangle Pitch through impact. You take a bigger backswing only to give yourself more time to accelerate the club head (when you are ready for speed), but that does not change the way you move through impact. You will *always* swing the club head and rotate through impact as in the Iron Triangle Pitch.

When the correct motion becomes easy and comfortable, tee balls up and hit very soft shots with little club head speed. Practice slowly and perfectly, and gradually shift your focus away from your mechanics and to the target. Don't let contact distract you. Just hit lots of balls and your contact will improve automatically. As you improve, add speed gradually, but never allow your swing to deteriorate under the pressure of speed. Speed should reflect competence, not strength or athletic ability.

GETTING THE BALL TO THE TARGET

I want you to push the club through impact in the correct direction so that the swing send the ball to the target. The swing's the thing. The ball is secondary to the direction of the swing. The ball just gets in the way. Once you're making the right swing, the only variable left in actually sending the ball to the target is be where the club face is aimed at impact. If the ball goes right, the club face was aimed right. If the ball goes left, the club face was aimed left. Adjust by using your hands and arms, just like steering a car, to rotate the club face either more or less through impact to get the desired direction. More on that later. Start with a twenty yard wide target, and try to hit balls within that area. As you improve, make your target smaller.

Then you are ready to hit pitches with the ball on the ground. Use **pitching address**. Contact is simply a matter of too low, too high, or just right. Don't give contact too much thought. It's just a matter of practice. Keep adjusting. Allow your wonderful mind to learn from the feedback contact gives you. When you hit the ground before the ball, that's called a "fat" shot. The adjustment is to swing higher next try. When you hit the top of the ball and roll it, that's called a "topped" shot. The adjustment is to swing lower. Golf is not rocket science, folks. Just keep adjusting and learning. And when you hit a particularly awful shot, laugh it off. Don't take this game too seriously.

As soon as you are able, find out what distance you can consistently hit sand wedge shots with the Three Quarter backswing. Use that distance as a benchmark and then adjust the backswing length to hit those pitch shots which are between Iron Triangle backswing and Three Quarter backswing lengths. Pick out balls on the range to use as targets. Go through your pre-shot routine (**See it**, **Feel it**, **Do it**) and change targets each shot. You need to get so good with your pitches that you can put the ball to within ten feet of the target all day long.

WATCH OUT FOR THESE MISTAKES

TOO MUCH BACKSWING
A larger backswing than the distance requires will cause you to decelerate on the down swing. You'll have trouble with contact and distance control. Keep it short and sweet.

LUNGING AT THE BALL
This is really just a spine angle change. Make sure you do not allow your head to drop down during the down swing, or you will experience what I call "ground effect;" the classic fat shot.

IRON TRIANGLE BREAKDOWN
This is a biggie. If you push the club head down through impact (thumbs down), you should not experience this flaw. But if you experience technical difficulty, spend a lot of time on pitching until you never see this flaw again. Iron Triangle breakdown also occurs on the backswing. Golfers often set their wrists and bend their elbows rather than turn their shoulders to start the backswing, adding more moving parts to their swing and making consistency and distance control unnecessarily difficult. Keep your entire golf game as simple as possible. You'll play better and run into fewer on course "meltdowns."

Congratulations!

Recognize the fact that you know what you are doing, and that, while you will still have to practice the mechanics of pitching, it's time to spend more of your practice time concentrating on the target, rather than on your swing. Remember. The object is to master the mechanics so that you can move on (graduate, if you will) to playing golf.

I certainly realize that there are a lot of mechanics to learn in golf, and I've done my best to help you learn the proper mechanics throughout this book, but you must make a clear distinction, and it's not so easy, between golf and golf mechanics. Mechanics are your ABC's, golf is writing a novel.

SECTION 2

THE LONG GAME

While the full swing (long game) is more difficult to learn, it is also the easiest part of the game—once you learn it—because there is only one full swing while there is an endless variety of short game shots.

Once you get through this section, it's time to stop listening to your friends' thoughts about the swing and stick with what's in here until you learn it. There are no short cuts. In this section, I'm going to give you a fundamentally sound concept for the swing that you must understand and internalize in order to execute. The golf swing is not a bunch of positions that your body must conform to. It is a concept that is derived from the way the club works. It's important to realize that the golf club is what counts—it's the only thing that hits the ball. Focusing on body positions or anything other than the club will distract your attention from what counts. There is no substitute for club head awareness.

If you've been trying to relearn your swing for a while, chances are you have already taken all of your attention away from the club, because that's exactly what most golf instuction has taught you to do. It's no wonder nobody really gets any better at this game! Listen. The club is the only thing that matters. Focus on swinging the club in the right direction and all those body positions you hear about will fall into place quite nicely. The photos you'll see are stop action (I'm sure you already knew that). While they show where the club should be at a specific point in your swing, they don't reflect the fluidity of the swinging motion. The photos do, however, illustrate my overall swing concept, not positions I try to attain. Don't focus on body parts, focus on the club. If your swinging the club in the correct direction, your club will look a lot like mine on your downswing although our body positions may look very different.

4
THE FULL BACKSWING

The feature of this book that I like most is how we build your golf game starting with the putt and ending with the full swing. The full swing relies upon the same fundamentals you learned in the short game section, but adds a longer backswing to provide more acceleration. Completing your swing will be easy because your fundamentals are so solid by now. Realize that you'll have to grind a bit at first, but your efforts will be rewarded with a fine golf swing.

Your backswing has a great impact on the quality of your downswing. Although you don't hit the ball with your backswing, a good backswing will certainly help make the downswing simpler and more consistent. Go slowly and correctly and be patient. It won't take long, and the payoff is worth the effort. A good backswing depends upon a good turn, and so we will start with the turn.

THE IMPORTANCE OF A MODEL

Having a clear swing model in your head (and sticking to it) is essential to your learning and continued improvement. There is so much information out there that golfers go to the course with several different swings in their head and can't decide which one to use. This indecision causes a lack of trust and, of course, the inability to focus purely on sending the ball to the target. Learn your swing once, and then use it for the rest of your life. You *will* have to fine tune it from time to time, but do not change your basic swing concept ever! This swing works, and it's simple. You just have to practice it until it becomes yours. You will need some sort of feedback (video is best) so that, when you are getting closer to the model. By the way, another pitfall to avoid is to judge your progress while you are progressing. Keep in mind that the model is about the club, not body positions. I guarantee that you're going to look different from me, but your club certainly should do something very similar to mine. You can only notice improvement in retrospect, and so you must be patient with (and non-judgemental of) yourself while you learn. You are on the right path. Stick with it and enjoy the ride.

Ignore all the swing theories, hot tips and gimmicks out there, and let yourself learn this extremely efficient method to the point of ownership. Then turn your attention to the target and send the ball toward it. Don't worry about contact. You'll learn to make good contact automatically. The effort to hit the ball is what destroys most golfers in the first place. From day one, golfers concern themselves almost entirely with hitting that little ball, completely oblivious to the fact that they have to send it to a target. So they improve their ability to hit the ball, but not their ability to play golf. It doesn't have to be that way.

Here's what you need to do...

7 STEPS TO GOOD GOLF

1. **Choose a good model for your game.** All learning occurs through a model. The model in this book is as simple as it gets and, most importantly, it works.

2. **See the model clearly in your head.** Study the model until you can see the complete motion in your mind's eye. Know where the club is supposed to be throughout the motion. Know where *you* are supposed to be. You must have no "blind spots" in your view of the model.

3. **Become the model.** Practice until you get a very clear feel for the swing. use video! Feel alone will take you far longer than using video to check where you actually are as opposed to where you think you are. This will take some time. Sorry, I cannot tell a lie.

4. **Use your swing to send the ball somewhere.** Introduce a ball only after you can consciously control the club (put it in the right place). Separate mechanics from golf. Swing to the target and watch what happens. Think "Hmmm, that's neat, let's send it over that way a little more." Practice becomes preparation for play.

5. **Trust yourself and play.** Stop working on your swing and use it. Focus on the target and send the ball there. Play Golf.

6. **Decide how good you want to get, and commit to a practice and play schedule that suits your goal.** The better you want to get, the more time you will have to spend. This might actually be step one.

7. **Make sure you spend at least one-half of whatever practice time you have on the short game.**

As far as the first five steps go, it is important, imperative actually, that you go in order. Most people go straight to Step 5, and never do get very good at the game. They end up giving up in frustration, thinking that golf is too difficult for them. Golf is not rocket science, it just has to be approached properly.

I don't mean to imply that this is going to be a cake walk for you. You are sure to have your ups and downs, but you can now take a more long-term view of your golf game, with the understanding that you are on the right path to good golf. And that's a whole lot better than floundering away with no clear idea of what you are trying to do in the first place. Be patient, and choose to have fun learning and playing. Play at learning. Play at practicing. Play at playing. Don't work at playing. We already work enough.

THE TURN

Most of the problems golfers have stem from not turning properly. When you make a poor turn, the club never gets into good position at the top of the backswing, and poor position at the top is almost impossible to recover from. Another neat feature of this book is that my students rarely have problems with the turn after they learn pitching, but I still want to make it clear, just in case you ever run into problems.

KEYS TO A GOOD BACKSWING TURN:

At the top of the backswing:

Important: It is Ok for your head to move as much as two inches to the right as you make your backswing. Do not try to keep your head perfectly still. Doing so may cause you to make a poor turn. That said, I should add that up and down movement is not a good idea.

1. Spine tilts slightly to the right.
At address position, your spine tilts slightly to the right. At the top of your backswing, your spine should still tilt to the right. The correct feeling is that your spine is the center of your swing and that you turn around your spine. You want to maintain your spine angle throughout your swing.

2. Left shoulder is lower than the right.
A line across your shoulders is perpendicular to your spine, right? Imagine the letter "T." That's what your shoulder line and spine look like. When your shoulders turn, they will remain perpendicular to your spine. From address position, your shoulders "seesaw" around your spine. The left shoulder is lower on the backswing and the right shoulder is lower on the downswing.

3. Left shoulder is behind, or at least even with, the ball.
How far you turn is a matter of flexibility. You may find that, due to a lack of flexibility, you cannot get your left shoulder to the ball without lifting your left heel off of the ground. In this instance I suggest allowing the left heel to come up a little, but no more than necessary.

4. Your weight is firmly on your right leg.
It is vitally important that you maintain the flex in your right knee as you turn to make the backswing. If you do not, your weight shift will be thrown off, and you will invite a whole bunch of problems into your swing. Your right leg is the main support of your backswing. As you turn back to the right, your weight should move to your right heel. Your right knee must maintain its flex in order to receive your weight. You want to feel like your upper body is leaning over your right leg just a little. Remember. Don't intentionally shift your weight. It should shift as a natural result of a good turn.

Watch your hip movement. Your hips should rotate as though you had a barbecue skewer right on up through your body in place of your spine. Do not let your hips slide to the right or left.

> Your legs are the foundation of your swing. Just as a your house needs a solid foundation, so does your golf swing. Your right leg is the main support of the backswing and your left leg is the main support of the downswing.

ONE GOOD TURN...

Left shoulder behind the ball and lower than the right. Weight firmly on braced right leg. My upper body appears to be leaning ever so slightly to the right, because I have maintained the spine angle that I had set at address. Practice your turn regularly. If it's not right, neither is your swing.

The Level Turn

Standing straight up, rest the club on your shoulders. If you can, rest it across your shoulderblades.

Turn your shoulders back to the right as on a backswing. Keep the club on both shoulders and allow your weight to shift onto your right heel. Your turning shoulders will cause your hips to turn also.

Check for these keys:

1. Try to get your left shoulder over your right foot.

2. As you turn back, your left knee is pulled in toward your right knee, with your left foot preferably flat on the ground.

3. Your weight has moved to the heel of your right foot. Feel that your right leg is "loaded" with weight.

The club should move parallel to the ground throughout this drill. Because you are standing straight, your spine is perpendicular to the ground. Your shoulder line is perpendicular to your spine, therefore your shoulder turn is **level** (parallel to the ground) in this drill. This condition will change as soon as you get into address position.

Now turn forward.

When you finish, check for these four keys:

1. Your left leg totally straight and holding almost all of your weight.

2. Your right hip above your left foot if possible.

3. Your right foot up on the toes, almost weightless.

4. Your spine should still be straight. There should be a straight line down the front of your body from your chest to your left foot.

I realize that doing turn drills is not all that fun, but if your turn is not correct, you're in for big problems. Start each practice session with these drills to warm-up. You'll probably play better than without doing them, and you'll improve the quality of your golf swing at the same time. That's a pretty good deal!

THE LEVEL TURN
Shoulders remain level (perpendicular to your spine) throughout. Try to keep your eyes straight ahead of you on the way back, but let them move forward, as though following the ball's flight, on the way forward.

DRILL

THE ADDRESS POSITION TURN

Now try the same drill from address position. Because you have inclined your spine at address, your shoulder turn is no longer level to the ground, but on an angle which is still perpendicular to your spine. Your left shoulder, therefore, ends up lower than your right on the backward turn, and your right shoulder ends up lower than your left on the forward turn. Make sure you still have that straight line down the **front** of your body at the finish, as above. That's very important.

FRONT VIEW AT ADDRESS

BACKWARD TURN: Left shoulder low; weight firmly on right leg; spine tilts slightly to the right.

FORWARD TURN: Straight line down the front of the body; right shoulder low; left leg straight, supporting almost all your weight.

SIDE VIEW AT ADDRESS

BACKWARD TURN: Maintain flex in right knee; spine angle is the same as at address.

FORWARD TURN: Hips face the target; right foot up on toe and weightless; spine angle is consistent.

DRILL

THE BELLY BUTTON TURN

Insert the butt of the club into your belly button so that it is perpendicular to your stomach, and take hold of the club out on the shaft so that your arms form the Iron Triangle. Using only your shoulders and hips, with zero hand and arm action, turn to the right, keeping your feet flat on the ground, until you can turn no more. The club should still be perpendicular to your stomach. Now turn forward. Again, the club should still be stuck in your belly button and perpendicular to your stomach. Remember to keep your right leg firm on the backward turn. On the forward turn, stop and check your finish.

Once again:

1. Your left leg should be totally straight and holding almost all of your weight.

2. Your right hip should be as close to above your left foot as possible.

3. Your right foot should be up on its toe, almost weightless.

4. There should be a straight line down the front of your body from your chest to your left foot.

BELLY BUTTON DRILL
Keep the club shaft perpendicular to your stomach as you turn your body. Don't use your hands at all, other than to hold onto the club, of course.

THE FULL BACKSWING

Start at address position and go to your Three Quarter Backswing. Your full backswing is almost complete from here, all you need to do is finish your turn and lift your arms a little. Your position at the top sets you up for the downswing. You can either make the downswing difficult or you can make it easy, all by where you put your arms and the club at the top. The full backswing checkpoints are as follows.

1. Left shoulder points at or behind the ball.
You know that already, but let me make it clear. You must make a good turn to make a good golf swing. It's that simple.

2. Left shoulder lower than the right.
Do not *try* to get your left shoulder down, that may cause a spine angle change. Your address position should make the left shoulder low condition automatic. Maintain your spine angle.

3. Weight firmly on your right leg.
Maintain the flex in your right knee. Your right leg is your body's support structure on the backswing.

4. Left arm is across your shoulder line (perpendicular to your spine) and quite straight. Right elbow points down toward the ground.
With your left arm across your shoulder line, you can start your downswing by extending back and down as we have already discussed. If your left arm is above your shoulder line, you'll have to make a loop in your downswing to get the club on the correct path. If your left arm is below your shoulder line, your swing will come too much from the inside, causing you to hit the ball too far out to the right. Your left arm should be as straight as you can make it without forcing it straighter than it wants to go. If it bends a little, that's Ok. Just don't let it collapse on you. Similarly, don't try so hard to get your right elbow pointing down that you become rigidly tight; your swing will look good, but it won't work!

5. Club shaft is just about parallel to the target line.
I could get real technical here, but I won't. I do not think it is vital to have the club shaft perfectly "on-plane" (parallel to the target line) at this stage of your game.

6. Right elbow is bent about 90^0, club shaft and left arm form 90^0 angle.
These are the **power angles**—most of your power comes from straightening these two angles. Watch out for over-bending your right arm. You can cause your left arm to break down, as well as get your right elbow into bad position.

7. Right forearm points just about straight down to the ground.
How close you get your right forearm to straight down depends upon your flexibility. The closer you can get to straight down, the easier the downswing will be. Just as with the straight left arm, do not force anything. Forcing leads to undue tension, which will ruin even the best swing.

AT THE TOP

AT THE TOP, FRONT VIEW

Spine tilts slightly to the right, as it did at address; left shoulder is behind the ball; right elbow is bent just about 90°, creating a gap between my hands and my head.

AT THE TOP, SIDE VIEW

Left arm across shoulders; right elbow points nearly straight down; right knee remains flexed; spine angle is the same as at address, making the left shoulder lower than the right (note angle down left side).

AT THE TOP, BEHIND VIEW

This view provides a better look at the right elbow at the top. Notice that, from this view, the right elbow appears to be in front of my chest.

IMPORTANT

I have certain physical limitations different from yours that will make our swings somewhat different although we try to reach the same position. Once again, do not force your body. Freedom from excess tension is more important than duplicating my position exactly. Come as close as you can to the model, but stay within your body's limitations. Golf's hard enough already. You don't need to fight yourself too!

Watch Out for These Mistakes

Be on the lookout for these mistakes, they can do a lot of damage to your swing.

The Reverse Pivot

Caused by a poor turn or straightening the right leg, weight does not shift properly to the right leg on the backswing. Rather, the weight actually moves to the left foot at the top (note how I am leaning over my left leg). Sometimes caused by attempting to keep the head rigidly still during the swing.

Overswing

Often caused by over-bending the right arm at the top. My left arm has bent considerably. My hands have gotten behind my head, narrowing my arc. I'll lose power and have more difficulty making solid contact from here.

Club Shaft "Laid Off" at Top

"Laid off" is golf lingo for the club shaft pointing well left of the target line at the top of the backswing. Usually caused by over rotating the arms on the backswing or a handsy take-away, this position makes the downswing extremely difficult. It is better to err to the other side of the target line, called "crossed-over."

Severely Bent Left Wrist

The back of your left wrist should be relatively flat at the top of the backswing. Getting the left wrist into this over-bent position places the club face in an abnormally open position, resulting in shots that fly far to the right of the target. Sometimes caused by excessive rotation of the arms at the start of the backswing.

5
THE DOWNSWING

Here comes the most important, most misunderstood, and most confusing part of the game. Why is the downswing so difficult? Ben Hogan said that you could do the opposite of everything you could think about the swing and come pretty close to a good swing. I think he was correct. The problem is that it's very difficult to maintain your focus on what you are doing during the half second in which the downswing occurs.

You must realize that, to play the game well, you have to have a downswing thought or key or image—*something* has to be going on in your head while you swing the club. Further, it had better be the right thing or you'll be spending your time looking for the ball in the trees. And, if you want to play well at all, it had better *not* be the ball!

Rather than have just one chapter on the full swing, I have decided to separate the backswing from the downswing because I want you to think of them as two different swings. That will help you understand and execute the transition from backswing to downswing.

The Arc of Approach

Let's talk first about *where* you need to swing the club, and then we'll continue our discussion on *how* to do it. The golf ball goes where you hit it. It doesn't know what kind of clubs you use, and it doesn't know if you are tall or short, weak or strong. It doesn't even know if you fall down after you hit it. Your success in golf is directly related to the quality of your downswing. It is very important to understand that you must consciously swing the club toward the target on every shot you ever hit if you want to be able to control where the ball will go. Don't confuse swinging the club *toward the target* with swinging *along the target-line,* they are two very different paths. The **Arc of Approach** is the path (it's not a straight line) the club head will travel when swung the way it was designed to work. The **target-line** is the (straight) line from the ball to the target.

The golf club does not swing along the actual target-line for long at all, even in the best swing. Rather, it moves more in a circular fashion around your body. I call this semicircular motion through impact the **Arc of Approach**, and it is fundamental to your understanding and mastery of the golf swing. The commonly heard instruction, "swing straight back and straight through," couldn't be more wrong. The photo below shows the Arc. In fact, if you do indeed swing the club along the Arc both back and down, you will end up looking very similar to the pictures in this book. The only thing you'll have to learn is straightening the Power Angles and you're ready for action.

The **target-line** is the solid line. Looking down the target-line, everything to the left of the target-line is *inside,* and everything to the right of the target-line is *outside.* Since I'm standing inside the target-line and swinging a long stick, as I make my backswing, the club naturally comes back to the inside (which many golfers do automatically), and should return to the ball *from inside, out* (which terribly few golfers *ever* do). That's the way both you and the clubs are designed to swing.

The Inside-Out Arc of Approach

The solid line represents the ball-to-target-line, while the dots show the Arc that the club head must travel to send the ball to the target. The ball-to-target-line is obviously very different from the Arc of Approach. When you swing the club, forget about the target-line and the ball and focus on the Arc of Approach. Swinging the club down the Arc is what will propel the ball along the target-line. For all full swings, your motion is *down the Arc.*

Inside Outside

BACK, DOWN, AND FORWARD

Now that you know about the Arc of Approach, let's talk about how to get the club on it. We began our discussion about the downswing in chapter three, and here we will continue it.

Understanding that the downswing's job is to swing the club head in the direction that will send the ball toward the target (down the Arc) is only part of the battle. The ball is the real problem. It will try to steal all your attention, leaving you unable to focus on where you are swinging the club. Listen. You *can't* try to hit the ball. I know that sounds crazy, but you have to just let it get in the way of your swing. The number one problem golfers have with this game is that they are so overly concerned with hitting the ball that they forget there's a place to hit it toward. They swing the club as though their only intention is to hit the ball. The club never does travel toward the target and neither does the ball. And they wonder why! Listen. If your goal is to hit the ball, you'll never play this game well.

The **transition** is the change of directions from backswing to downswing. There is a very slight pause at this point that serves two purposes. First, as you "set" (stop) the club at the top, you'll be more aware of its position. And secondly, it helps you avoid rushing the change of directions and starting in the wrong direction. From there, push the club back and down toward the Arc to start the downswing. Keep pushing back and down until that motion turns into forward and down the Arc.

The transition is the key to the downswing. Whatever you do at this point *must* result in the club swinging on the Arc of Approach to the target. Anything you do that causes the club to swing away from the Arc will work against you. Traditional golf instruction has led to exactly this problem. For years, golfers have been trying to follow instructions that won't work. Those days are over!

Making a great downswing is not physically difficult at all, you just have to be able to pay attention for at least as long as it takes to make your swing.

BACK, DOWN, AND THEN FORWARD

This photo shows the transition. *Back* is away from the target. That's part of what makes golf so difficult—it's just the opposite of what you think you'd want to do. *Down* is toward the ground, and *Forward* is toward the target.

My hands and arms don't just start the downswing, they make the entire downswing happen by simultaneously pushing the club head back and down onto the Arc of Approach and continuing to push the club head through impact until back and down turn into forward toward the target. Let the club come around on its own. Don't try to force it. Be patient.

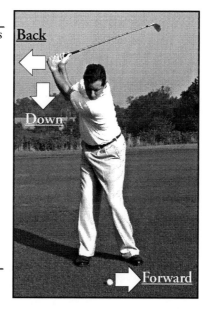

THE SWING PLANE MODEL

WARNING: This is advanced stuff and may be a little too technical for the new golfer. I have included it for golfers who have been at the game for some time, and need a "proof," if you will, of why I teach the golf swing so differently from traditional instruction. For those of you who have been at this for a while, this may be exactly what you need. You're probably trying something that almost certainly can't work.

Golfers have searched for the secret of the golf swing since the game's beginnings. The answer has been right in front of our noses all the time. The club is the master model of the golf swing. The *club* dictates how it should be swung! We've spent so much time looking at different body parts and weight shift and elbow positions and on and on that we've forgotten (ignored?) the only thing that counts: the club.

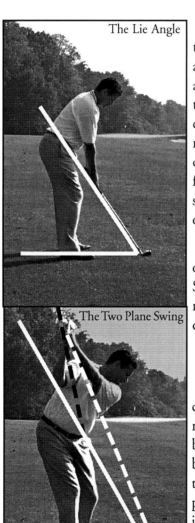

The Lie Angle

The Two Plane Swing

THE LIE ANGLE

The Swing Plane Concept is based on the design characteristics of the golf club, specifically the **lie angle**. The lie angle is formed between the club shaft and the ground at address. In this position, the club is perfectly square to the target. To hit great golf shots, we must return the club as close to this position as possible. The ideal golf swing is represented by golf club testing machines that swing the club at this angle throughout the swing so that the swing forms a perfect circle. The machine hits virtually perfect shots time after time because the club never varies from its original, intended, design angle.

The **plane board** (pages 108 and 109) is a representation of the lie angle that provides a guide for the golf swing. Swinging the club along the board ensures that we always return the club to its original position—the way it was designed to work—just like a machine.

THE TWO-PLANE SWING

Because of our anatomical design, our hands and the clubshaft *automatically* shift from the original plane to a more vertical plane (black line) as we complete the backswing. You see, the plane runs (roughly) through our belt buckle, while our arms are attached to our body up at the shoulders, making it impossible to remain on the same plane throughout a full backswing. Because this plane shift is inherent to the way our body moves, *we don't feel it.* Since we are unaware of the shift, we don't realize that we have to shift back to the original plane on the way down. Instead we swing right at the ball, on a third, much more vertical, plane than the original. The club is not designed to work when swung more vertically than it's intended design, and so it doesn't work. We slice, pop-up, pull, hit fat, and lose considerable distance. Worse yet, try as we might, we improve frustratingly little.

Now that you are aware of the golf swing's inherent plane shift, you can do something about it. You are now prepared to make your practice pay off. Listen. Whatever you do as you start the downswing had better make your hands and the club return to the original plane. The easiest way to achieve this is to *push* the club there using your hands and arms. Any other move (and there are so many suggested moves that it's silly), will cause the club to move away from the plane first, requiring you to figure out a way *in mid-swing* to get back on-plane or worse, to remain above-plane or "over the top" throughout the swing. Swinging over the top means that the club *cannot* swing along the plane. Instead, it will cut across the plane on its way through impact. You'll be swinging the club contrary to its intended design, and you'll have to compensate by making another error or you'll have no chance of sending the ball to the target. Good luck!

The benefits of getting the downswing back on-plane are great. Both accuracy and distance improve because you are swinging the club the way it was designed to work. The on-plane club moves more level through impact, transmitting your energy toward the target (the slicer's swing heads down into the ground). Swing speed, and therefore distance, is increased as the right forearm (the major source of power) and the club shaft add to each other as they act on the ball from the same plane. The club travels at ninety degrees to its axis of rotation (the spine) which is required to achieve maximum speed. Lastly, the on-plane swing makes squaring the club face at impact nearly automatic as centrifugal force and gravity combine with the design of the club to do the work for you. All you'll have to do is simply allow as much rotation as the shot you want to hit calls for, rather than having to force the club face to return to square.

Any swing can work *if* you're able to compensate for your errors, but most of us have neither the ability nor the practice time available to attempt to groove such mid-swing corrections. To that end, I suggest you use the simplest, most effective way to swing a golf club. I'm not saying that all golfers should look exactly the same, but all golfers should comply with the laws of physics and the design of the club, don't you agree? Yes, you *could* initiate the downswing by rotating your hips forward as is so often taught, but that move only makes it more difficult to get on-plane. Accordingly, great players *body positions* vary widely from player to player, but their *club movement* on the downswing is strikingly similar.

Perhaps the greatest benefit of all is that once the on-plane swing becomes your model, you need never again search for the latest hot tip, gimmick, or quick fix. You simply continue to move closer to the model swing. Every bit closer you get, you control the ball better *and* you understand why. That's fun.

It's very important to understand that if the club shaft is more horizontal than the original plane angle (called "flatter"), the club can still work very well, particularly with the longer clubs, but if it is more vertical than the original angle, it will not.

THE PLANE TRUTH

The plane board shows the simplest, most efficient way to swing the club. Because the club travels along the target-line as much as possible, contact is assured and control and power are maximized. All I must do is make the transition from the top of the backswing back to the plane and I'm set.

Yes, great golf comes out of lesser swings, but those swings are more difficult to execute and to maintain. Such swings also require a great deal of athletic talent and practice time to control.

The beauty of the Swing Plane Model is that the closer you get to the model, the better you hit the ball. Period. When you "lose it," you have only to check your swing on video and compare it to this, and you will instantly know what to do. It is far better to know what's right rather than try to figure out what's wrong.

ADDRESS
Starting out right on target. Club shaft and hands are on plane.

THE TWO PLANE SWING

Now that you see that it is not possible to remain on the same plane throughout the full swing, your understanding of the golf swing will become much clearer.

It is the start down that will make or break you. Ben Hogan called it a "crossroads." If you take the wrong road, you can't get where you want to go.

By understanding that you must return to the original plane before you head for the ball, you can rule out all the other theories of how to start the downswing because they can't possibly result in returning the club to the original plane. Your confusion is now in the past.

By the time I reach the top of the backswing, I have shifted from the original plane (white) to a secondary plane (black).

FULL BACKSWING (UP ABOVE PLANE)
Left arm across the shoulder line. I'm well above plane and need to get back down on it if I intend to swing toward the target.

My hands move down the secondary plane on their way back down to the original plane.

PUSH BACK & DOWN (TO THE PLANE)
Club shaft flattens (tilts) back toward its original angle as I push the club back down on plane.

2

HALFWAY BACK

Club shaft, hands, right forearm, and right elbow are all on plane.

The club leaves the plane as I 3 lengthen my backswing for power, but my right elbow remains on-plane. Note: Hands in front of right biceps muscle indicate correct position.

THREE-QUARTERS BACK

I'm trying to stay on plane, but my body will not let me. Right elbow only is on plane.

PLANE AND SIMPLE

Try as I might, as I complete my backswing, I cannot remain on the board. I'm forced to "shift" above it onto a new plane.

Looking at photos #4 - #6, you can clearly see that to get my downswing back on-plane, I *must* push back and down. If I turn either my shoulders or hips first, my hands and the attached club will move out to the right and farther away from the board. The club will then slice across the plane as it moves through impact. That's the slicer's swing that 80% of all golfers use to hack it around the golf course.

In reality, the club shaft will become 6 flatter than the original plane because it must be perpendicular to its axis of rotation (your spine) to reach full speed. It will still align with your right forearm, however.

HALFWAY DOWN

Club shaft, hands, and right forearm have returned to original plane. The key to golf.

7

IMPACT

Looks a lot like address, except that my swing has forced my hips to open slightly.

WHAT DO ALL GREAT BALL STRIKERS HAVE IN COMMON?

Note the similarity in the position of my *hands* in photos 3 and 5. They are in front of my right biceps muscle on the backswing and again on the downswing. The more closely your hands come down to the plane, the better you'll strike the ball.

Many lesser ball strikers (even among the pros) return only the club head back to the plane, while their hands remain considerably above-plane. While good shots can and will be produced with such a swing, more manipulation of the club face is necessary, making consistency much more elusive.

THE SWING CIRCLE, PART 1

In a way, the swing is like a circle—what goes around comes around. ***Pushing the club back and down will force the club's motion to** automatically **turn forward.** Once *back and down* becomes *down and forward,* the club will automatically rise up to a fully extended followthrough, despite the fact that you are still pushing down. Try it right now, without a ball, just to prove it to yourself.

PUSH THE CLUB BACK AND DOWN

If you swing the club on the correct path, maintain your posture, and return to the Triangle through impact, you're on a collision course with the ball. You don't even have to look at it to make contact because you can't miss!

When I say push back and down, that's exactly what I mean. Don't pull the club down with your left hand. Don't try to hold any angles. Don't drop your right elbow to your side. And, above all, don't turn!!! All you need to do is use your arms and hands to push the club back and down. Your pushing motion will turn your body around for you. If you do turn forward to start the downswing, you will instantly move the club away from the Arc—the classic slicer's move.

THE LOW POINT OF THE CIRCLE

Please notice that, as the circle suggests, the low point of the swing is reached AFTER impact. That's extremely important for solid contact with the irons. Remember to push the club down even after impact.

DOWN & OUT

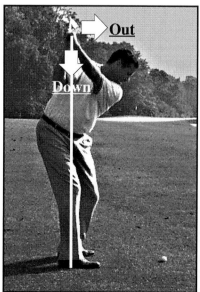

The straight line drawn from my hands is the direction in which you must push the club—down toward the original plane. In the photo to the right, you can see exactly that move. Because your arms are attached to your body, your downward effort will not continue straight down (your effort should remain in that direction, however). Rather, your swing will automatically become more circular and travel along the Arc of Approach.

The other option, Out (to the right), is the direction we want to avoid like the plague. If you turn your hips or shoulders to start the downswing, you will instantly send the club Out rather than Down, making it nearly impossible to swing the club toward the target (Hello, slice!).

THE DIFFERENCE BETWEEN DOWN AND OUT

The start down is the most important move in golf. Now that you understand the Swing Plane Model, you can see why many of the conflicting ideas you've heard about how to start the downswing *can't* work. Those ideas are probably your reason for buying this book. Whatever you do *must* move the club **down** toward the plane. If your first move sends the club **out** away from the plane, you've got serious problems. The easiest, most obvious, way to get the club on-plane is to push it there.

DOWN—ON-LINE TOWARD THE TARGET

Notice how both my hands and the club are moving closer to the original plane as I start down. Pushing *back and down* to generate the downswing is the most direct route to the original plane. Keep it simple!

Above plane at the top..........Pushing back and down........Toward the original plane...To an *inside-out* approach.

OUT—OVER THE TOP—THE SLICER'S SWING

Using body rotation (shoulder or hip) to start the downswing causes the hands and the club to move **out** to the right. My hands move down parallel to the plane, but not on it, which results in the club cutting across the plane rather than traveling along it. Anything you do that causes the club to move away from the plane (or the Arc—same thing) will result in severely diminished control and power: Slices, pop-ups, pulls, lack of distance, and deep divots all result from this move.

From the same backswing......Turning to start down.......Forces hands and club out...To an *outside-in* approach.

The Swing Circle, Part 2

Knowing about the Swing Plane Model and trying to swing accordingly may or may not lead to actually making the right swing. In many cases, the *feel* of a good swing is so foreign that it takes serious determination and discipline to make the necessary changes. What makes learning the golf swing do difficult is that the right swing feels like it's going in the wrong direction. All I can say is: Get used to it!

In order to give students a clear image or feel for the right swing, I revisit the Swing Circle idea found on page 110. This is a different, even more important, point of view than the Swing Circle, Part 1. This circular image can help you return your hands to the original plane and get the club head on the proper path on the downswing. Think of this circle, see it in your mind's eye, and swing the club along it, and you've pretty much got the golf swing mastered. Amazingly, simply by having this circular image of the swing, students instantly make a better turn and achieve a much better position at the top of the backswing and, best of all, make a phenomenally better downswing.

Close your eyes and visualize the circle using your mind's eye while making slow swings, and try to feel the club head traveling along the circle. When you can really feel the weight of the club head in your hands, tee up some balls and totally ignore them while you concentrate only on your circle throughout the *entire* swing. If the ball gets in the way, great! If not, forget it and try again!

Very important note: Don't try to finish the circle. Let the club come around after impact all by itself as a result of your swing's momentum. Forcing the club to come around to the finish will ruin your swing. In fact, I seldom, if ever, teach the finish.

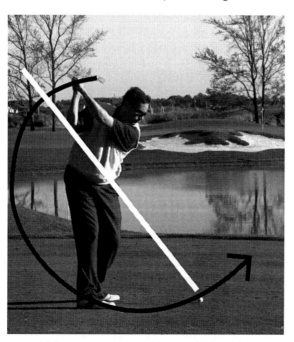

THE SWING IS A CIRCLE

Feel the head of the club as you swing along your circle and your hands will return to the original plane and the club will swing right over the Arc of Approach. The Swing Circle may very well be the most important image in this book.

THE ANGLE OF ATTACK

Many golfers search for more club head speed because they believe that more speed equals longer drives. The truth is: more club head speed is not necessarily the answer. Worse still, trying to swing faster might just ruin your swing.

The first thing I want you to understand is that the **angle of attack** (how level to the ground the club moves through impact) has more to do with distance than pure club head speed. If your club moves downward through impact, you will transfer less energy to the ball because the ball will slide up the club face rather than compress against it. (Of course, your swing concept has everything to do with your angle of attack.) We can liken this to hammering a nail. The best way to drive the nail is straight through it. Have you ever missed or glanced off the side of a nail? Doesn't work very well, does it? I hate when I do that! The same holds true for driving a golf ball, and so I submit to you that your lack of distance will not be cured by swinging the club faster—only by swinging it better. Take a look at some of the LPGA Tour players. Many women hit the driver considerably farther than the average male golfer, yet they seem to swing much more slowly, and certainly with much less effort. Well, it's all about the angle of attack.

Now then. I told you that so that I could tell you this: The only way to create a level attack is to have the club head approach the ball from the inside-out, which is what I'm trying to teach you. I'm sure you've heard about inside-out before and have tried hard to do it, but there is a major reason why you've been unable to own it.

LOOKING FOR POWER IN ALL THE WRONG PLACES

Using the wrong power source will make it nearly impossible to return your hands to the plane and create an inside-out, level angle of attack. I call them "off-plane pulls," because they pull the club and your hands away from the plane. You've probably heard all sorts of ideas on how to generate power, but most are dead wrong, meaning, they'll ruin your swing. Drive your legs toward the target; turn your hips or shoulders; coil; pull the club down from the top of the backswing with your left arm; shift your weight toward the target—I think that about covers most of the wrong ideas—will ruin your swing. Now that you know that a level attack is the way to longer drives, let me tell you why the above ideas don't work: They all make it nearly impossible to create that all-important, inside-out swing. All of those ideas force the club to come down at a much more vertical, downward angle, which works great for wedges but horribly for drives. But wait, there's more.

You can try your heart out to do what I'm telling you, but if you accidentally (meaning, you aren't aware of it) use one of the above, very common, power genera-tors, you'll *never* get it. I'm not a strong person, but I can generate nearly 80% of my full swing speed using only my right arm and hand. What's more, using only my two hands and arms and trying to "zero out" all other movement, I can achieve 100% of my full club head speed! I found that out using a laser club head speed detector. **Club head speed comes from your hands and arms and distance comes from a combination of club head speed and level angle of attack.** Don't ever forget that!

DOWNSWING KEYS

1. **The Swing is a circle. Push the club along the circle.**
   The design of the golf club dictates that the swing should be circular. You must swing the club in accordance with it's design or it won't work for you. Feel that you are getting the club head as far away from you as possible as you push. The wider your Arc, the more room you have to accelerate *and* the straighter the club moves through impact. A wider arc, therefore, gives you both more power and more control.

2. **As you push back and down toward the circle, the club shaft angle "flattens."**
   Once again, note the change in club shaft angle as we move through the three photos below. Turn your head and watch, or look in a mirror. See it happen. If you see the club shaft between your shoulder and neck half way down, you missed the circle. You'll have to feel as though you are pushing down and *behind* you more to correct yourself. It will probably feel awkward at first, but don't let that discourage you. What you have to feel to get the club swinging properly may not feel good for awhile, but that doesn't make it wrong!

3. **Club shaft lay over the right forearm.**
   If your downswing is properly round, your club will look just like this. This is the "on-plane" condition we are striving for. At this time, the clubshaft should either point at the ball, or slightly "outside" of it (see photo). Get out the video camera and check yourself, getting the club here could be the key to your swing.

SET FOR TAKE-OFF	PUSH BACK AND DOWN	CLUB SHAFT ON RIGHT FOREARM
Left arm across the shoulder line. Try to keep your left arm "soft." Swing the club head right from here (begin releasing now).	Right arm extends back and **straight** down, while hands push the club. As I extend down, the club shaft flattens toward the original plane angle.	Hands are on-plane, club shaft covers right forearm and is perpendicular to my spine. Shoulders and hips just begin to feel the arms pull them into motion. Swing the club on the proper arc, and your club will look just like mine.

4. Impact. Push the club down the Arc of Approach.

The power angles you set at the top of the swing (wrist set and right elbow) have been "released" (straightened) back into the Iron Triangle. Although my arms have straightened fully, I have released a great deal of the tension in my hands as though I were throwing the club through the ball. That's essential for creating maximum speed. Just as in chipping and pitching, the hands are slightly ahead of the club head and the club shaft leans forward.

5. Followthrough.

Extension toward the target. But of course!

6. Finish in balance.

Balance equals control. Allow the club to finish the swing purely as a result of the momentum generated in the swing. Never force the finish, just let it go.

Here are two excellent thoughts to keep in mind:

Feel as though you are swinging through water.

Keep pushing the club all the way through impact. Right now you should be going very slowly, but with the idea that you will gradually accelerate from the top of the backswing, all the way through impact.

Don't hit *at* the ball, push the club through it.

The effort to make contact can cause you to change your swing. You want to be only remotely aware that the ball is even there while you make your swing. The idea is to swing the club and let the ball get in the way.

FULL RELEASE AT IMPACT
You can't see it from here, but my arms have straightened fully, returning to the Iron Triangle at impact. My forward motion has caused my hips to turn slightly toward the target.

FOLLOWTHROUGH
Hips and shoulders are pulled around as I continue pushing forward toward the target.

FINISH
Perfect balance, the sign of total control.

POWER STORAGE AND RELEASE

At the top of the backswing, you set two power angles that represent stored energy. They are the angle between the club shaft and left arm (wrist set), and the right elbow bend. The club head gains speed as you straighten these angles, and reaches full speed when the angles become straight lines. The **release**, then, refers to straightening out these angles. Many golfers equate rotating the club face through impact with the release, but that's not accurate. (I call that "rotating the club face.")

Contrary to popular instruction, you want to begin releasing immediately as you start the downswing. In fact, the release *causes* the downswing. "Hold the angle" and "release late" are instructions which are actually the opposite of what great players do. Witness the bending of the club shaft at the top of the backswing in nearly all great players. The bend comes from pressure against the shaft. The pressure comes from the hands pushing against the shaft (releasing). The only way to bend (also called "load") the shaft is to release. With that said, the wrist angle release will, in most cases, occur automatically as you push the club, so you probably won't have to worry about it. Definitely ignore all instructions along the line of "hold the angle."

Here's the drill: Complete your backswing and stop at the top. Gradually straighten your right arm back and down to push the club along the Arc of Approach. Come to a stop at impact, where the club shaft and left arm form a straight line. The key to the release drill is to continue pushing the club down along the Arc of Approach using your hands and arms while your hips and shoulders and body move only as a response to the pushing motion.

RELEASE THE CLUB DOWN THE ARC OF APPROACH

Begin releasing (straightening the power angles) right from the start of the downswing. Shoulder and hip rotation should occur only as a response to the release. Feel the pressure of your hands against the club shaft and your right arm straightening in a piston-like motion. Although it may seem too easy, please do this drill. It will teach you nearly everything you need to know about the downswing. Keep in mind that your hands should be loose, while your arms (particularly your right arm) supply most of the effort.

In the truest sense of the word "release," you want to feel as though you are letting go of the club as you approach impact. Most golfers do just the opposite—squeeze the club, just when they need to release it. I often have students literally throw their club down the fairway to give them the proper feel of releasing the club through impact.

This drill exaggerates the release to the point that you will most probably find the Power Angles become fully released (straight lines) before impact. That's fine for now. You are not using any arm speed yet, and so the release is early. But when you notch up your arm swing to full speed, the release will be just right. In fact, the only way you *can* release too early is if you don't accelerate your right arm all the way through impact. Keep in mind that your motion needs to be smooth and needs to flow. You should feel your arms just start to pull your hips into motion as your hands approach impact. Feel the momentum of the club head pull your arms down the fairway.

I know that this concept would seem to create casting, but I have had tremendous success at fixing students' casting problems with exactly this concept. Casting is nothing more than a deceleration of the arms. If you release all the way down, the arms and hands keep moving and this "lag pressure" you have applied to the club shaft creates sustained acceleration.

It's very important to realize that the vast majority of your power comes from your right arm and hand—not your legs, hips or weight shift. If you'll just pick up a club with your right hand and swing it around, you'll find that you can swing it as much as 80% as fast as you can with both hands. Try that, just to prove it to yourself. Use something that measures club head speed just for fun. Trying to get power from other sources (legs, shoulders, hips) will throw your swing in the wrong direction.

POWER RELEASE AND THE MISUNDERSTOOD CONCEPT OF "CASTING"

Want more power? Straighten the Power Angles faster. Casting, which is often considered a swing flaw, is nothing more than releasing the Power Angles out of synch. If your wrists unload faster than your right arm, the wrist-set Power Angle will straighten before impact, robbing you of speed. The answer is to speed up the arm action, not delay the release. The key is to release both Power Angles so that you accelerate the club head *through* impact—not just into it.

DRILL

THE PUNCH SHOT

Up to this point, we have been stopping at the top of the backswing and then starting the downswing. We will now add the **transition**, which is the smooth change of directions from the backswing to the downswing. I want you to go, ever so slowly, to the top of your backswing. As soon as you reach the top, start the downswing just as slowly and continue on through impact to the followthrough, as in the Push Drill, and stop. Be very aware of the completion of the backswing and the transition. Did you feel your right arm extend with piston like action? Did you feel your shoulders turn first? Did you move your hips first? Did you flatten the club shaft on the way down? Did you extend forward toward the target? Open up your feelers.

While you do this drill, you must be certain that you are doing it correctly. As I've already said, that's why I want you to go slowly. You must learn to flow from the top of the backswing through impact and onto the followthrough.

The mechanics must precede the feel. Learn to produce the correct mechanics first, and then learn the *feel* of the correct mechanics. At first, this drill will help you learn the correct mechanics. Eventually, you will own the mechanics and will be ready to reproduce them by feel. Don't put feel first. You'll end up doing a great job of learning the wrong thing.

THE PUNCH SHOT

Slow but continuous motion from address to the followthrough. The followthrough will be a little higher now, due to increased momentum gained from a longer swing. (I've gone very slowly for these photos, creating insufficient momentum to carry me to a higher followthrough).

At first, I want you to start down in the slowest motion possible and then gently and gradually accelerate through impact toward the target. Avoid trying to hit the ball far right now, and focus your attention on swinging the club in the correct direction. As you master this drill, you can add speed gradually, but always with a slow start and continuous acceleration through impact. Hold and check your followthrough for accuracy.

Know what you are working on and evaluate only that. Right now, you are working on making a slow, flowing, perfect downswing with the intention of swinging the club toward the target. As I have said, contact is just a matter of practice. Don't give it a thought. Keep swinging correctly and contact will come naturally. *It is inaccurate to evaluate the quality of your swing based on the feedback you get from contact.* Soon enough, you will reach a level where you can and should work on ball flight, but not yet.

Let me make something clear. Do you remember when I said that some motions create other motions? Well, in the downswing, your shoulders are not *totally* motionless, they have to move some, but that movement is *passive*, and results directly from the *active* movement of your arms and hands. Your arms are connected to your body, so when one moves the other must respond. To swing toward the target, you must move your arms and hands and let the rest of your body respond as it needs to. You will have to be very aware of the transition to get it right. Feel, for certain, that your arms and hands control the downswing, and that your body's rotation forward occurs well after you start down.

The Punch Shot can be used on the golf course as a fantastic iron shot when your distance to the hole leaves you between clubs. Hit the longer club a little softer and Punch it! You'll see that shot on the TV quite regularly. I've had students play the best golf of their life by hitting punch shots all the way around the golf course.

THE BALL GOES WHERE YOU HIT IT!

Note the forward extension in the far right picture on this page; it's going toward the target, right where I want the ball to go. Doesn't that make sense?

THE FINISH

You are now ready to complete your swing. But really, *you* don't complete the swing. Momentum, along with total relaxation, does it for you.

The **finish** (what most people call the "followthrough"), is a product of what comes before it, and greatly depends upon the club head speed you generate during your swing. When you increase your speed, your finish will take care of itself. Incidentally, the reason a Punch Shot doesn't have a finish is that you use only 75% of full speed: You don't swing fast enough to create enough momentum to cause a finish.

The finish is absolutely not a position to strive for in itself, because trying to arrive in a certain position takes your mind off of the important part of the downswing. Allow your swing to continue onto the finish, but don't *try* to finish your swing. Let the club head pull your arms and hands around. That said, if you do things right, you will end up very similar to the checkpoints below.

Finish Checkpoints:

1. **Perfect balance. Balance *is* control.**

2. **Left leg straight with almost all of your weight on it.**

3. **Hips face the target. If you are very flexible, your right hip may be closer to the target than your left.**

4. **Club shaft touches the back of your head or your neck.**

5. **Right foot up on the toe, with almost no weight on it.**

6. **Right shoulder is a little lower than your left.**

Well what do you know, we are done with the full swing. Practice it until it becomes a simple matter of feel, then you'll be able to repeat your swing with amazing consistency. Remember that only perfect practice makes perfect.

STORE ENERGY   RELEASE ENERGY   FINISH IN BALANCE

STORE AND RELEASE ENERGY

Conserve energy on the backswing, and expend it on the downswing. It's very common to expend energy on the backswing through muscular tension and too much speed. You don't want to do that. The backswing is smooth and unhurried and the downswing is a smooth and gradual acceleration to full speed (full release of energy). The club just floats to the finish. You want to feel as though you were going let go of the club and throw it down the fairway. Don't rush. Accelerate too abruptly, and you'll run out of speed before impact.

The Full Swing

The following full swing sequences put together all that you have learned thus far. Try to imagine the flow of movement from frame to frame.

Facing View

IRON TRIANGLE AT ADDRESS

Balanced and poised for action.

IRON TRIANGLE BACKSWING

All shoulder turn to this point. No wrist or elbow bend yet.

PUSH BACK AND DOWN

Notice the lack of hip and shoulder motion in photos 5 and 6. My hips and shoulders are patiently waiting for my arms to pull them into action.

THREE QUARTER BACKSWING
Wrist set causes right elbow to bend. Arms lift club up toward the top of the backswing.

FULL BACKSWING
Shoulders have turned 90^0. Right arm is bent about 90^0. Spine tilts slightly to my right (the reader's left). Right knee is still flexed.

IMPACT
The return of the Iron Triangle, aka. a full release. Club shaft leans slightly forward, hands in front of club head.

FOLLOWTHROUGH
Keep pushing the club forward toward the target. The overall purpose of the golf swing.

FINISH
Balanced and totally relaxed. Weight is firmly on left leg.

FULL SWING SEQUENCE

TARGET LINE VIEW

ADDRESS

Spine is straight. Arms hang down from shoulders. Perfect balance.

IRON TRIANGLE BACKSWING

Shoulder turn to here. Right knee bend is the same as at address.

PUSH BACK AND DOWN

Notice how still my shoulders and hips are in these two photos. My arms have not yet caused them to turn toward the target. Club shaft has flattened and covers the right forearm in photo 6.

THREE QUARTER BACKSWING

90° wrist set. Hands are in front of my right biceps muscle. Note the similarity to photo 6.

FULL BACKSWING

Left arm across the shoulders. Right forearm points nearly straight down. Right knee is still flexed as at address.

IMPACT

Looks a lot like address, doesn't it?

FOLLOWTHROUGH

Says it all. The club is headed right toward the target.

FINISH

Balance. If you do everything right, the club shaft will point through your ears.

FULL SWING SEQUENCE

FORWARD VIEW

ADDRESS
Hello, ball!

IRON TRIANGLE BACKSWING
All turn.

PUSH BACK AND DOWN

Note the club shaft behind my back in photo 6. Notice the flattening of the club shaft from photos 4 through 6.

THREE QUARTER BACKSWING
All set to lift arms up to the top.

FULL BACKSWING
Left arm across the shoulders—hands are outside my right shoulder.

IMPACT
Hips are slightly more open than at address.

FOLLOWTHROUGH
Throwing the club right at the target.

FINISH
Balance, but of course.

Full Swing Sequence

Rear View

Address

Have a friend give you a little push forward and backward to check your balance.

Iron Triangle Backswing

No arm or wrist bend yet. Shoulder turn has not yet pulled my hips and left knee into motion.

Push Back and Down

Body remains calm and passive while right arm straightens and wrists uncock to accelerate the club head.

CAUTION: Objects in rear view are smaller than they appear. Honest!

Sometimes, I crack myself right up!

THREE QUARTER BACKSWING

Shouder turn has caused hips to turn and left knee to point toward my right. Full wrist set.

FULL BACKSWING

Right arm is bent 90⁰. Note position of right elbow and hands. Right leg supports.

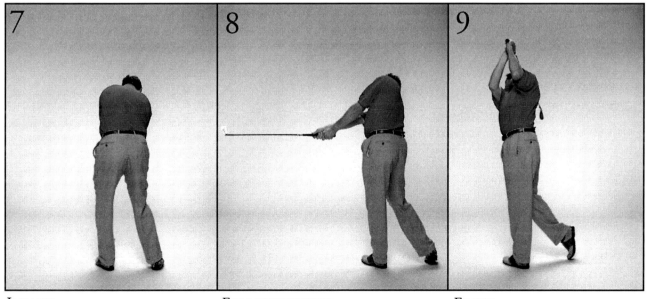

IMPACT

Still pushing the club down even after the ball is gone.

FOLLOWTHROUGH

Still pushing, extending toward the target. Down has turned into up automatically.

FINISH

Balance mainly on the left leg.

The four keys to the swing

These are the four things you *must* get right in your swing. Please study these and practice them until you own them. When you video tape or look in a mirror, you should use the target line view most of all, as it shows you what you really need to see.

1. Left arm across the shoulder line

At the Top

Left arm is across (parallel to) shoulder line. Left shoulder is just about over top of right foot.

Try saying the four keys as you slowly swing the club. Say them to yourself (or out loud, if you dare) as you do them. "Left arm across the shoulders." "Push back and down." "Extend to the target." "Finish." Swing only as fast as you can be consciously aware of, and totally in control of, the motion.

2. PUSH THE CLUB DOWN THE ARC

STRAIGHTEN THE POWER ANGLES TO MOVE THE CLUB
Straighten the Power Angles by pushing the club back and down the Arc.

 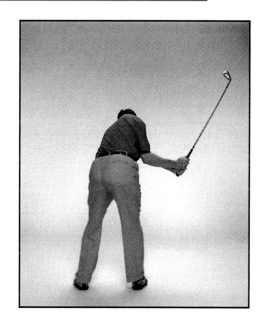

The four keys to the swing

3. Extend to the target

The Followthrough

Keep pushing the club down and forward, toward the target. The ball goes where you hit it, right?

4. FINISH BALANCED AND AT EASE

THE FINISH

Perfect balance is a sign of total control. Body facing the target, weight on left foot, club shaft through the ears. The position, itself, is not as important as maintaining your balance.

WATCH OUT FOR THIS MISTAKE

THE PULL VERSUS THE PUSH

THE PULL—AWAY FROM THE TARGET

It looks like I'm trying to pull the club toward myself and away from the target. Now that doesn't make any sense, does it? Yet this is the move through impact that I see in most golfers.

THE PUSH—TOWARD THE TARGET

My extension toward the target is obvious. The intention behind the shot is clear. If I were throwing a ball underhanded, my right arm would extend forward toward the target in much the same way.

THE INFAMOUS CHICKEN WING

The left elbow bent tightly against my side and the club shaft pointing way left clearly show that I had no intention of sending the ball to the target.

LOOK MA, NO ELBOWS!

You can't see my elbows or the club shaft. Soon after this point, the club shaft will appear somewhere above my left shoulder.

THE GOLF IMPERATIVE!

When working on mechanics, strive to swing the club perfectly. Learn what a good swing feels like. When playing golf, forget about *how* to swing, and focus on *where* to swing. These may seem to be the same thing, but they are very different, indeed.

MECHANICS ARE SELF-CENTERED. GOLF IS TARGET-CENTERED.

DON'T CONFUSE THE TWO.

Some students are so dedicated to improving their Golf Swing that they forget to Play GOLF. They work on mechanics at the range *and* on the course. That's the wrong approach if your goal is to play better GOLF. While mechanics are important, learning to PLAY GOLF is what it's all about. Golf is the name of the game, not Golf Swing. If I had only one thing to say to my students, it would be this. Keep the target in mind and swing the club toward it. That's how you PLAY GOLF.

Congratulations!

When you are ready, and you'll know when you're ready, pat yourself on the back for a job well done and realize that it's time to let go of your mechanical thoughts and just play. Remember, that's the goal of this instruction. Learn it right, and then forget it. Now, I don't want you to think that you are finished working on your swing. But as soon as you are ready, you want to divide your practice time between working on your swing and hitting the ball to the target. They are not the same, you know.

6
FULL SWING DRILLS

As you can probably guess, I firmly believe that the fastest way to improve your golf is to combine knowledge of what to do and why to do it, with drills that teach you *how*. These are more of my favorite drills that I use to help students learn really fast. This short section is included to supplement what you have already learned. They pinpoint specific problems and can help make your practice more productive. I urge you to do all drills with the ball teed up.

Listen. Don't try to learn the lessons these drills teach immediately, and don't knock yourself out doing them. Just run through them during your practice sessions and allow them to gradually educate your body to want to do the right things. The drills take time to incorporate their lessons into your swing. Don't rush. Be patient.

Golf has a way of letting us know exactly where we stand relative to where we would like to be. If you do the drills, but have difficulty maintaining your balance or making solid contact, that's no surprise. It just means you are not "there" yet. As you improve your mechanics, your contact will improve also.

DRILL

GRADUAL ACCELERATION

This is my number one drill to train and maintain your swing. The purpose is to create total awareness and control of the entire golf swing. I am absolutely amazed by how well and how quickly this drill works.

Make a backswing in slow motion and stop at the top. Start the downswing in slow motion, and gradually accelerate through impact. Avoid any abrupt acceleration. When you are ready, change directions without stopping at the top (add a smooth **transition**). The key is to start the downswing in *very* slow motion so that you are absolutely certain that your are pushing the club back and down, and that your hips and shoulders are motionless.

Feel the straightening of your right arm as your hands move down. Keep pushing back and down (the club shaft should flatten if you swing over the Arc) in slow motion until your hands are about belt high as in the second photos, top and bottom. Once there, gradually accelerate through the ball, toward the target, to a full finish. Remember that your arms will pull your body around through impact. Look at my right arm's extension toward the target in the third photo, top row. That's forward!

Say the moves out loud as you do them. "Backswing." "Push back and down." "Extend to the target." "finish." Keep the club moving at the same speed as your voice.

Start out hitting fifty yard 7 Irons until you can pure it more often than not, and then move up to seventy-five yards until you own it. Keep increasing the distance by twenty-five yards until you reach full speed. A full speed swing will still use gradual acceleration, only the overall speed will be greater. A slow, smooth transition and constant acceleration to full speed through impact are necessary for all golf shots.

DRILL

THE OBSTACLE COURSE

   Accurate feedback can be hard to come by when you're out on the range. Aside from bringing a video camera along to your practice sessions, the Obstacle Course is the best source of feedback you can use to tell you where your swing is going.

   Arrange two head covers as shown, giving yourself just enough room to make your Arc of Approach into and through impact, but not enough room to get away with the wrong path. If you hit either head cover, you know you were on the wrong path. Immediate feedback. I love that! You *must* be able to concentrate on swinging the club along the Arc *while you swing*. It's one thing to *think* it and another thing to *do* it! I use duct tape or chalk to show the path and often have students look at a spot on the tape instead of at the ball. At first, they can't believe they actually make contact without looking at the ball. Then comes the revelation: "I don't even have to look at the ball to hit it?!" Their entire game improves as they give less and less attention to the ball, allowing them to focus on where they are swinging the club. Don't let your mind go blank while you swing, and don't let your mind get absorbed by the ball. *CONTROL YOUR CLUB!!!*

THE OBSTACLE COURSE

With just enough room to swing the club on the Arc of Approach, the Obstacle Course provides instant feedback if I happen to miss the Arc. Students are usually amazed to find that they hit the ball better when they pay no attention to it (I'm not!). The ball just gets in the way.

THE INSIDE-OUT ARC OF APPROACH

If you swing the club properly, the club will travel right over the tape and avoid both head covers without problem. The only way for the ball not to go to the target is if the club face angle is not square. Now we've narrowed ball flight control down to the last variable: club face control. See Practicing Golf—Ball Flight Control for a complete discussion on what influences the golf ball's flight and how to work on ball flight control.

KNOW WHERE TO SWING!

Note the use of two parallel alignment clubs—one near my feet to help me aim correctly, and one near the ball showing the ball-to-target line and the use of duct tape to show the proper Arc of Approach. The difference between the Arc and the target line is a critical concept that most golfers fail to understand.

THE THREE FOLLOWTHROUGHS

Like the Three Musketeers, these three drills should stick together. Work on these three followthrough checkpoints at each practice session to encourage extending all the way through impact toward the target. Practice the Three Followthroughs until this extension becomes the only way you know how to swing the club, and then practice 'em some more.

The key to stopping the club at the proper point is to swing with only enough effort that you run out of gas by that point. The first drill requires very little speed and the other two require increasingly more speed. Avoid swinging too fast and stopping the club like you ran into a wall. That will cause you to decelerate before impact, and you *always* want to accelerate the club through impact.

When the Three Followthroughs become natural *and* you swing on the correct Arc, your bad shots will be very playable. That's the key to hitting lots of fairways and greens. Add a good short game and you're looking at shootin' par.

FOLLOWTHROUGH #1 RELEASE BACK TO THE IRON TRIANGLE
Although it's not exactly address position, it's close enough to illustrate the point. You must straighten out your arms back into the Iron Triangle to play good golf. Nearly all good players get to this position, but the average golfer's arms are bent in an effort to pull the club through impact. (That's what causes topped shots.)

FOLLOWTHROUGH #2

The momentum gained by pushing the club a little faster through impact will carry you to Followthrough #2, aka. the Push drill. My arms haven't even thought about bending at this point—bending would force my club to swing away from the target.

FOLLOWTHROUGH #3 ARMS ARE STILL STRAIGHT

Here is the real Punch Shot finish. If your goal is to push the club toward the target, your arms will not bend until you reach this point. This is the true end of the golf swing. The finish is simply relaxation from this point.

DRILL

THE LEVEL SWING

If you have really tried, but are having difficulty with your golf swing, The **Level Swing** may really help you out. This drill is designed to help you teach yourself the proper movements of the swing from a position that makes the swing a little clearer to see than normal address. It's sort of a baseball swing, with a couple of particulars. Do this drill correctly, and you may find that your problems are solved by combining this drill and its companion, the Foot High Swing, which turns the Level Swing into a golf swing.

Hold the club chest high with your arms rather straight. The club's **leading edge** should point straight up and down. Swing the club back and rotate your arms until the **club face** faces the sky.

Check for these backswing keys:

1. **Shoulders level (parallel) to the ground.**

2. **Left arm straight across the shoulder line and level.**

3. **Club shaft level.**

4. **Club face leading edge level.**

5. Your right elbow should point down to the ground and should not touch your side.

After you have the backswing correct, swing **up** to the imaginary ball that is chest high. The downswing is very similar to a home run hitter swinging for the fences; it's low to high.

Your arms need to rotate the **leading edge** back to its original, pointing up to the sky, position when it gets straight out in front of you (impact), and then continue to rotate until the club face faces the ground at the finish.

The **Level Swing** is exactly the same as a golf swing but by standing up straight, you will be able to see more clearly where you want to be in your swing. By doing this drill until you can flow continuously from backswing through finish, you can create excellent habits, and all you will have to do is bend down into address position and let those habits take over.

Important!!!

In order to swing up to the imaginary ball, you will first need to lower your arms toward the ground just a little to give yourself room to swing up. That is just like starting the downswing by extending your right arm back and down.

SWINGING UP

It is very similar to the baseball swing, as I've said, but a topspin forehand in tennis and throwing a hook in bowling are also helpful images. Notice how much lower my right elbow is than my left in the first photo. You want to see something similar in your real swing.

THE FOOT HIGH SWING

This drill makes the transition from the Level Swing to the golf swing easy. Set up for the Level Swing, then bend from the hip joints and lower your arms until the club head is one foot above the ground. You will be in close to full swing address position, only standing a little straighter, with the club one foot above the ground.

Make your backswing just as in the Level Swing. The only difference is that at the top of the backswing, because you have bent over into address position, your left shoulder will be lower than your right, and your left arm, the club shaft and club face will be level with only your shoulders, and *not* the ground. It is very important to realize that, due to your bent over address position, the club shaft will no longer be level with the ground at the top of the backswing, rather it will point up toward the sky.

When you start the downswing, what used to be a low to high swing will become inside-out (on the Arc of Approach), just the way we want it.

It may help to think of the **Foot High Swing** as an *angled* **Level Swing**. The **Level Swing** is horizontal, while the **Foot High Swing** is angled. Make absolutely certain that you do not confuse the two drills. You can ruin your swing real fast. You must remember that the club will point up toward the sky on the backswing in the foot high swing.

The Foot High Swing also makes for a good pre-shot practice swing on the golf course. You will see some of the best players in the world make this sort of swing before or after a shot to remind themselves of the correct feel for their swing. It will remind you to swing on the Arc of Approach.

APPROACH THE BALL ON THE ARC, NOT ON A STRAIGHT LINE

Think of making your downswing very round through impact. That will help you get the idea of the correct shape of the swing. Swinging out to the right of the target can also help you generate the Arc.

THE SWINGING START

This drill will help you flow rhythmically through your swing. After you have gotten comfortable with (and good at) your swing, you will need to switch off your mechanical mind and allow yourself to use what you know. Try this to help smooth out the bumps.

1. Start at normal address position but hover your club above the ball by an inch or so.

2. Swing the club **forward** about three feet, and then smoothly start the backswing, and continue on just as a normal golf swing. The momentum of this **swinging start** will greatly reduce the friction in your swing.

FEET TOGETHER

Your hips should rotate above very stable legs during a golf swing and not slide back and forth. The lateral slide away from and/or toward the target (called a "sway") is a very common error that really hurts your ability to hit the ball solidly. This drill will: all but eliminate swaying; teach your legs to remain sturdy through the swing; and get your hands swinging the club head.

You will be amazed by how well you can hit the ball like this once you gain your balance.

Practice this drill every time you hit the range. It's good for you.

RIGHT FOOT OUT

This drill will help you zero out hip action so that you can work on the correct downswing. Practice this drill if you feel your hips moving first at the start of the downswing. It can also help you get the feel of swinging inside-out through impact.

Set up with the ball centered in your stance and pull your right foot back behind your left as pictured. You'll have to gain your balance at address, but don't worry about going off balance on your finish. This address position will "lock out" much of your lower body movement so that you can get your hands in control of the swing.

Through impact, feel as though you are swinging well out to the right of the target so that you approach the ball on the Inside-out Arc.

NO WAY TO SWAY

Swaying turns the ball into a moving object and makes contact more difficult. This drill not only eliminates the sway, it also inhibits early hip movement, and gets your hands and arms moving first on the downswing.

DRILL

LEFT FOOT OUT

This drill is designed to teach you how to properly support your weight on your right leg on the backswing. Similar to the previous drill, the Left Foot Out drill also makes it nearly impossible to start your downswing by sliding forward, toward the target.

Center the ball in your stance, then move your left foot back behind you and balance mainly on your right leg.

As you make your backswing, make very certain that your right leg remains rock solid, with your right knee in the same position that you had set at address. You may even want to try to "sit" or "squat" on your right knee just a little as you go back.

Swing down on the same arc I've mentioned. Your weight will want to shift to your left foot on the downswing: let it.

SOLID BASE

Many golfers have real difficulty properly training their right leg to support their body on the backswing. This drill does it for you. Just like the previous drill, this drill also helps prevent swaying.

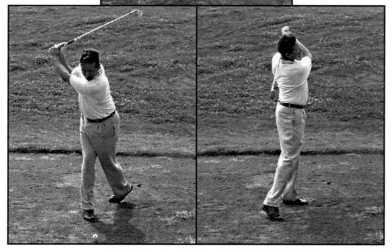

DRILL

RIGHT HAND ONLY

Here is a great drill to get the idea of swinging the club with your right hand and arm. Hold the club with your right hand only and make a golf swing. Hold your right biceps muscle with your left hand. Make sure you allow your right elbow to bend to a ninety degree angle at the top of your backswing. On the downswing, make sure you push the whole club back and down, don't just pull the grip down. *Feel* your right arm straightening back and down and the weight of the club in your right hand as you push against the club shaft. Do this drill often to create a clear image of what you will do on the downswing.

THE NUMBER ONE SOURCE OF POWER

I hit my 7 Iron 160 yards with both hands, and 130 yards with just my right hand. Hmmm. Makes you think, doesn't it? When I was starting to get pretty good at golf, I often heard "Pull with your left hand to start the downswing." That tip only made me slice the ball. If I was really with it back then, I'd have said "I'm right handed. Why would I ever want to swing the club with the other hand?" I can't even brush my teeth left handed.

SECTION 3

PRACTICING AND PLAYING
THE GAME

We are (finally) about to move out of the realm of golf technique and into the world of GOLF. In this section you'll learn to use your knowledge to create the shot you want to hit. You'll learn about the variety of shots the course will require you to hit, and you'll learn how to practice so that you really do become a real golfer, not just someone who plays at golf. At the end of the book is a troubleshooting guide that will help you if you get stuck.

7
PRACTICING GOLF

You are the teacher, and you *will* learn whatever it is that you teach yourself, so do your job well. Precise practice is far more important than the quantity of balls you hit. However, GOLF is different from practice, and you have to be able to move from golf swing mode, into GOLF mode if you want to play well. This chapter is here to help you make that transition.

Before I even begin, let me say that if you are still working on your grip, you are not ready to hit golf balls yet. If you still have problems with your backswing or downswing, you are not ready for golf balls either. Please get the mechanics out of the way (mastered to the point where your swing is as easy to execute as driving a car or riding a bicycle) before you worry about where the ball goes.

WHAT ARE ALL THOSE CLUBS FOR, ANYWAY?

The sand wedge is your short distance club. In addition to pitching, you will use this club with a full swing. Hit full shots with your sand wedge, and find out how far they fly. Then do so with every club in the bag. You need to find out your *average carry distance* (how far the ball flies in the air, excluding roll) with each club, so that you know which club to hit when you are, say, 150 yards from the hole. Learning your distances will take time, and before you can even consider distance control, you have to become proficient enough with your swing to make solid contact most of the time.

Once you find out how far your full sand wedge flies, let's say 75 yards, you'll use the sand wedge for all pitches and up to 75 yards. Once over 75 yards, it's time to switch to the pitching wedge which will take you from 75 yards up to about 100, or a range of about 25 yards over sand wedge distance. From the pitching wedge on up through the long clubs, the length difference between clubs becomes a fairly predictable ten to fifteen yards. Don't try to hit the ball farther when using longer irons. Swing the same and let the club do the work. The long irons can be more difficult to hit because they require quite a lot of club head speed to get the ball up high. If you find the 5, 4 and 3 irons difficult to hit, you may want to try a utility club, like a 7 or 9 wood, because the low center of gravity makes it easier to get the ball up. The larger head on these woods gives players more confidence as well.

Since you will hit more short irons than long irons during the course of a round, you should spend more practice time with the short irons.

You may find more success driving the ball with your 3 wood rather than your driver (1 wood). The driver is the least forgiving club in your bag and is too difficult to control for most people. As such, I often tell students to leave the driver in the trunk. Most players will find that the added height they get with the 3 wood actually results in more distance than they get with the driver, *and* the ball goes straighter. If you plan to use a driver, I strongly suggest that you get one with at least 10 and preferably 11 or 12 degrees of loft until you become an accurate, long hitter and the ball goes too high. I use a 9.5 degree driver.

Here's my set of clubs and the distance I hit each club on the fly.

Driver	260
4 Wood	230
2 Iron	210
3 Iron	200
4 Iron	190
5 Iron	180
6 Iron	170
7 Iron	160
8 Iron	150
9 Iron	140
Pitching Wedge	115 to 130
Gap Wedge	80 to 115
Lob Wedge	80 and all pitches.

This is the way *my* set works for *me*. These are *average* distances. Not the longest I have ever hit with each club, rather the distance I can safely count on every time I swing that club. You will get different distances with your set. The important thing is to find *your* distances, and don't try to equal your favorite touring pro's distances. You never want to press for distance with any club. Swing within yourself. Trying to smash a club longer than you are capable of results in some really neat looking shots, usually less distance and, almost always, higher scores.

Between these clubs I can choke down on the club or shorten my swing to take a little distance off if necessary. Notice the gap between the 8 and 9 iron. If I have a 145 yard shot, I will hold down an inch lower on my 8 iron and use a full swing to take five yards off my usual 8 iron distance. I can also use the three quarter speed Punch Shot to do the same thing and the ball will fly lower, making it very useful in the wind.

Posture

Your posture is very important in making your swing repeatable. Many golfers make the mistake of changing their posture as they change clubs. That is unwise. Your posture sets up all the angles of your swing. If you change your posture, you change your swing. You need to use the same posture for all clubs, and just stand farther from the ball as the clubs lengthen.

WEDGE   6 IRON   DRIVER

BALL LOCATION

Ball location has to do with where the ball is placed relative to your feet. We are going to make this as simple as possible. For all full shots, the ball should be placed within two inches of your left heel. To encourage the proper angle of attack into the ball, you will simply move your right foot either closer to, or farther from, your left. The ball remains in the same location, relative to your left foot.

The short clubs require a somewhat more descending blow, that is to say, a steeper angle of attack. You don't have to change your swing at all (thank goodness!). Just move your right foot so that your heels are about six inches apart. This ball location will place the ball at the low point of your swing so that you will automatically hit slightly downward on the ball. As you move up from the wedges through the set, gradually widen your stance as you take longer clubs. Your driver stance should have your feet shoulder width apart to encourage a flat approach to the ball.

One more comment about ball location. You must experiment a little to find out which works best for you. If you find your ball starting out too far to the right, move the ball a little closer to your left heel, and do just the opposite if it starts out to the left. Particularly, if the ball starts out far to the right of the target but has some draw (left curve) on it, moving the ball forward will help the ball start out on a better line. Of course, be sure that you are making a good swing before you change ball location.

Note that my left foot is turned out a little toward the target. I do so to allow my hips to rotate properly as I swing forward. Without turning the foot out, I can't finish my swing. Try that, especially if you aren't terribly flexible.

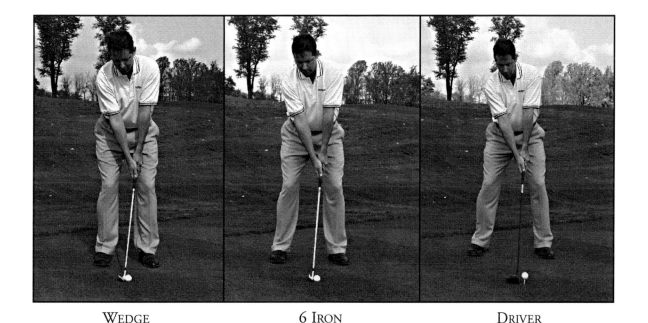

WEDGE   6 IRON   DRIVER

APPROACHING THE BALL AND THE WAGGLE

When you are preparing to hit a shot, you will have to move into address position. The approach to the ball is often overlooked, but it is still a very important link in the chain of events leading up to the swing.

AIM. READY. FIRE!
Aim the club face first, and then align yourself. A couple of waggles and you're ready to fire. Make sure that you keep moving while you ready yourself, it will help you stay loose.

The way you move to the ball can make it easier to align yourself to the target correctly. Aim your club face before you take your stance. Stand to the side of the ball and face the target to aim your club face. Facing the target in this manner helps your accuracy in aiming the club face *and* aligning yourself. Complete your hold first, before setting the club down to aim it. Then tilt your head up to get your eyes as parallel to the horizon as possible while you aim to and lock the target.

Take your stance while loosely moving the club back and forth over top of the ball in a miniature golf swing. This movement of the club is called the waggle, and serves two purposes. It helps get rid of shot-destroying tension, and it serves as a preview of the Arc of Approach. Many golfers freeze over the ball and get tighter and tighter until they can hardly swing the club at all. Waggle the club over the Arc to set the Arc firmly in your mind. Then try to swing the club in the same direction in which you waggled. Imagine orange paint on the bottom of the club and "paint the Arc" to help set it more clearly in your mind. The waggle will really help you make good swings.

Stand behind the ball and pick your target. Walk to the ball. Aim your club face first, then align yourself. Slowly look at the target while still waggling and settling into your stance. Then move your eyes slowly back to the ball. When your eyes come back to the ball, swing with only the target or the Arc in mind. **Note: Some students play better trying to swing over the Arc. Some fare better trying to swing toward the target. And some do best with the adjusted target. Try all three. It doesn't matter which one you choose, all three images are target oriented.**

ON YOUR ARC.
GET SET. GO!
Don't just wiggle the club around when you waggle. Use your waggle to fix the Arc of Approach in your mind, and make sure you swing along that Arc. Many students play better looking at some part of the Arc, rather than the ball. Try it. You'll like it!

WAGGLE BACK   WAGGLE FORWARD

CONTACT!

Let me first say that the ball is what messes people up in the first place. You try so hard to hit the ball that you forget about where the target is and swing only to hit the ball. You have to send the ball to the target!!! I don't really want to include this in here because I don't want you to become obsessed with contact, but I've included this page about contact just in case you are experiencing difficulty. Concentrating on contact completely removes the target from the picture. Once the target disappears, your cooked. Imagine playing darts without knowing where the dart board is. It doesn't work, does it?

As you practice, you gain experience in how to bring the club to the ball. You need to relax and be totally non-judgemental while your brain soaks up the feedback that contact (or lack of contact) gives you. You *need* make lots of mistakes right now, so don't get too excited about what you perceive as "bad" contact.

Take lots of practice swings and try to brush the ground without digging deep divots. Put a tee in the ground and try to hit it. When you can hit the tee repeatedly, put a ball on it. As you improve, lower the height of the tee progressively until you no longer need it. Hitting the ball consistently from the grass may take several days, weeks or months. Please don't rush the process. If you become frustrated when trying to hit the ball off the ground, put it back on a tee and regain your confidence.

Basically, contact is a no brainer. If you swing over top of the ball and miss completely, you've swung too high. Any time you hit a ball that rolls, you have swung just a little too high and contacted the ball above its equator. In both cases, swing lower. Try to hit the ground a little on the next try. If you hit the ground behind the ball, that's too low. Swing higher. I told you, this isn't rocket science. Adjust.

If you are hitting the ball extremely to the right with an iron, you may be shanking the ball. Take a look at the neck (hosel) of the club and see if you have ball marks on it. If you do, first make sure you are swinging inside-out, and then simply stand a little farther from the ball (more on shanking in Chapter 9). If you are swinging inside-out but hitting it off the toe, move a little closer.

At this time, you may want to play golf. Feel free to tee the ball up on all shots, except those near the green, until you are confident and having considerable success on the course. By the way, you can't tee the ball up in a tournament, unless you are hitting a "tee shot," but it's a great idea for now.

I highly recommend that you start with a par three course, then graduate to a longer, executive course. Then, when you are ready, go for the full size, championship course. Remember, the object is to have as much fun as possible. Don't go get yourself beaten up by a course that's beyond your capabilities. That's no fun at all.

THE RIGHT CLUBS FOR *YOU!*

By this time, you are ready to get clubs that fit you, if you haven't already. Basically speaking, you need to have the correct shaft length and flex, the correct grip size, and the correct lie angle. Many golf course pro shops now offer club fitting service, using one or more of the excellent portable club fitting stations offered by leading club manufacturers. These units have several different clubs with varying lengths, flexes and lie angles for you to try, until you find the one you hit the best. Incidentally, you do not necessarily need *new* clubs. If you like your present set, they can easily be adjusted to fit you. And that's a lot less expensive than a new set.

When fitting someone for clubs, I first look closely at their address position and posture, not just their height, to determine the proper length shaft. Then I check swing speed and, particularly for woods, look to see how much the student loads (bends) the shaft at the top of the swing. That helps me determine the right shaft flex. I check grip size by looking to see whether the left hand fingers rest against the palm rather than digging in or not touching at all. Finally, I have them hit a few balls from what's called a lie board, to find the proper lie.

Since most clubs come in only regular or stiff flexes, most of my students get the correct shaft. Tall players over six feet *may* need longer than standard clubs. Short players under five feet, six inches *may* need shorter than standard. Petite clubs are also offered by many club manufacturers for players under five feet.

The most important club fitting variable is probably the lie angle, and that should be done with a lie board which shows you where the sole of the club contacts the ground. I put duct tape on the sole of the club and have the student hit balls off of the lie board, which is just a flat board placed on the ground like a hitting mat. After the two balls are hit, I look at the sole of the club to see where the mark left by contact with the board, not the ball, is. If the mark is in the center of the sole, it fits. A mark out on the toe means the club is too flat, and will cause an otherwise good shot to go to the right. Conversely, a mark on the heel means the club is too upright, and will cause the ball to go to the left. Most clubs can have the lie angle adjusted to fit properly, but you must get to a lie board to find out what lie you need. Do not trust a finger tip to floor measurement. The lie angle you require depends more upon your swing than your height and arm length.

The significance of lie angle cannot be overstated. For every degree too upright or flat, the ball will go eleven feet left or right of the target on a 150 yard shot. To play well with clubs that do not fit you requires that you compensate in some way for the ill fitting equipment. Golf's hard enough. Get your clubs fit to you. A good club fitter or a competent PGA or LPGA golf professional will be able to help you find the right clubs.

BALL FLIGHT CONTROL

Control the golf ball and you will play good golf. Once you have mastered the correct club path, you will quickly learn ball flight control. The golf learning sequence goes like this:

1. Learn the pre-swing fundamentals (hold, stance, posture).

2. Learn the mechanics (how to's) of the short game and the full swing.

3. Learn ball flight control.

4. Apply your knowledge to the varying conditions of the golf course.

We're almost done! Now you're ready for step three.

There are two main factors that influence ball flight. They are the club path, and the club face angle. The **club path** is the direction in which you swing the club through impact, and can be either **inside-out** or **outside-in**. The **club face angle** is the direction in which a perpendicular line from the club face points at impact, and can be **open**, **closed**, or **square**. Let me restate the difference between inside-out and outside-in.

Stand behind the ball and look down the target line. To the left of the target line is inside, and to the right is outside. The opposite is true for left handers. When you take your stance to the ball, you stand to the left of, or inside, the target line. Right? Because you are holding a long stick in your hands, the club head must move inside the target line as you swing the club back. Therefore, the club should return to the ball from *inside* the target line, *out* to the target line. That's called an **inside-out** approach to the ball (the Arc of Approach). Everything you have learned so far has been designed to teach you to swing inside-out. Understand that not only are *you* designed to swing inside-out, so too is the golf club. Forget any ideas of swinging the club straight back and through toward the target on a full swing, you can't possibly do it. Trying to do so can only make the club *and* your body work against you.

INSIDE-OUT APPROACH
Allows me to swing toward the target through impact.

The **outside-in** approach to the ball is woefully common to amateur golfers. Due to a number of possible swing flaws, many golfers swing so that the club head approachs the ball from outside (right of) the target line and then across the line to the left. There is no way to swing toward the target! This approach to the ball can cause big problems in your golf game. The dreaded slice, shots pulled left of the target, deep divots, pop-ups, and loss of power are common to the outside-in club path. If you swing down the Arc, you have nothing to worry about.

OUSTIDE-IN APPROACH
To save yourself, don't try to hit the ball, hit the Arc instead.

You are rapidly approaching the stage where you can use ball flight as feedback to evaluate your swing. Knowing your ball flight laws makes it easy to adjust your swing (which you should not have to do very much) and the club face angle (which is easy but requires practice), to control the ball.

Here's how it goes:

BALL FLIGHT LAW #1

Initial direction is a function of the CLUB PATH.

When you make contact with the ball, the ball compresses against the club face. This compression allows the ball to "stick to" the club face and pick up the direction in which the club head is traveling during the time of compression. The direction of the club head is called the club path. The line of compression, refers to the direction in which the club head travels while the ball is compressed against it. The line of compression (which is a fancy way of saying the club path), then, determines the direction in which the ball starts out, immediately after leaving the club face.

BALL FLIGHT LAW #2

Curvature is a function of the CLUB FACE.

The curve on a golf shot is caused by spin applied to the ball by the **club face**. Your club face can be **square** (aimed straight to the target), **open** (to the right), or **closed** (to the left). The only way the ball can curve to the right is if the club face is aimed to the right at impact. Conversely, the only way the ball can curve to the left is if the club face is aimed to the left. A square club face will send the ball quite straight.

Note: These ball flight laws are not absolute, but they are extremely useful in learning to control your golf shots. If the **club face** is way off line, the ball will not have a chance to compress against it, and the ball will just slide off, hence the first law does not apply. However, if your hold is correct and you avoid "death gripping," the club, your club face should be pretty close to where it needs to be. As well, if the **club path** is way off, you can add curvature to the shot. I tell my students to ignore the really strange looking shots rather than try to fix them. You can't fix the bad shots. It's too late. Rehearse your good swing, and try again.

BALL FLIGHT LAWS QUIZ

1. What is the main determinant of the ball's **initial flight**?

2. What is the main determinant of the ball's **curvature**?

3. Ball starts left of the target and curves to the left. Was the **club path** inside-out, or outside in?

4. Ball starts right of the target and curves hard to the left. Was the **club face angle** open, closed, or square?

5. Ball starts left of the target and curves right. What was the **path**? What was the **face angle**?

6. Ball starts right of the target curves slightly left (draws) into the target. What was the **path**? What was the **face angle**?

7. Club face square to path. Does the ball slice, draw, or go straight?

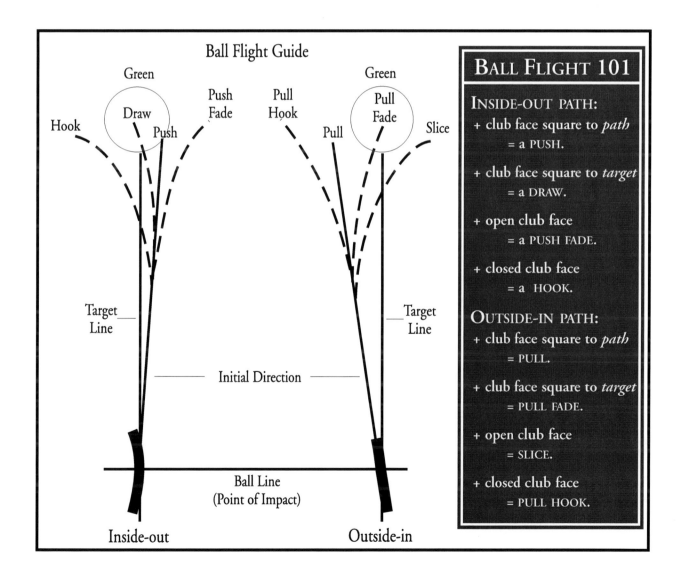

Ball Flight Guide

BALL FLIGHT 101

INSIDE-OUT PATH:
+ club face square to *path*
  = a PUSH.

+ club face square to *target*
  = a DRAW.

+ open club face
  = a PUSH FADE.

+ closed club face
  = a HOOK.

OUTSIDE-IN PATH:
+ club face square to *path*
  = PULL.

+ club face square to *target*
  = PULL FADE.

+ open club face
  = SLICE.

+ closed club face
  = PULL HOOK.

OK, here are the answers. Again, ball flight is pretty basic. The ball goes where you hit it. 1, Club Path. 2, Club Face. 3, Outside in. 4, Closed. 5, Outside in path, Open club face. 6, Inside-out path, Square club face; great shot! 7, Straight.

Understanding what makes the ball do what it does can really improve your golf game. When you understand what makes things happen, you can more readily make changes which will create the desired ball flight.

When you practice your ball flight control, make certain that you have alignment clubs down on the ground (see page 141 or 172) so that you take the variable of alignment out of the following equation:

$$\text{BALL FLIGHT} = \text{ALIGNMENT} + \text{CLUB PATH} + \text{CLUB FACE ANGLE}$$

You will do best to make alignment a given so that you can concentrate only on the path and the face angle.

You will do even better if you can make both alignment *and* club path given. That's what all the full swing instruction was for.

When you start the downswing by pushing back and down, the club will approach the ball from the inside just as it should. Therefore, your golf ball should start out slightly to the right of the target. Hopefully, the inside-out path is a given in our ball flight equation so that the only variable remaining is the club face angle. Let me state that another way. Before you can really learn how to bring the club face into impact squarely, you *need* both alignment and club path under control.

The ball flight goal for now is to create a right to left shaped curve, called a **draw**. A draw is the natural ball flight for the inside-out club path. The club is designed to rotate from open to closed through impact, which is why nearly all great players fight a hook. Line up to the target, and try to hit the ball two yards to the right of it. Carefully watch where it goes. Do not judge the shot as either bad or good, just note where the ball started and adjust your path appropriately on the next shot. Keep your ball flight laws in mind. If the ball starts out immediately to the left of where you are aligned, your path was outside-in. Check your start down. Make sure that you start the downswing by extending your right arm back and down. Feel that you are swinging the club a little to the right of the target. If the ball starts out slightly to the right of the target, your path was inside-out. That's what we want. If you have trouble getting the ball started in the right direction, fool yourself into the correct path by aiming at the actual target, but swinging the club 10, 20, or more yards to the right. It's surprising how strange the correct path can feel.

Next, watch how the ball curves. If the ball curves to the right (a slice), the club face was open at impact. If the ball curves to the left significantly (a hook), the club face was closed at impact. The more severe the curve, the more significantly the club face was open or closed. A "draw" is a mini-hook, and a "fade" is a mini-slice. What you need now is to educate your hands so that you can make the ball do whatever you want. Do try to get the ball curving left consistently, because that means the club is rotating properly through impact.

EDUCATED HANDS

You must control the club path and the club face as the club moves through impact if you want to tell the ball where to go. I call this process "educating your hands." You will continually improve this skill as long as you play golf. There is no substitute for educated hands, and there has *never* been a great player who didn't have great hands.

Educate your hands by rotating your arms—not just your wrists (like turning the wheel of a car) to rotate the club face through impact. Our first goal is to make the ball curve left every time. If the ball curves left, at least you know you have one of two ball flight control factors working. If the ball curves left too much, that's just fine—you can always rotate a little less.If the ball curves right, you won't know whether you made a bad swing or just left the club face open, but when the ball curves left, that means the club face is doing its thing and the ball will basically go in the direction in which you moved the club through impact. That's the key to your improvement!

SQUARE AT ADDRESS

When you first start making the ball curve left, you will find that some (or more) of your shots start out to the left of the target and then curve farther left. That's because your club path is heading outside-in. No problem. Keep the ball curving left and then move your club path more from inside-to-out to make the ball start out in the right direction. You may have to feel like you're swinging far to the right of the target to send the ball to it. That's ok. Feel is not real.

Try to hit big hooks by over-rotating the club face, and then make the ball slice to the right by under-rotating, leaving the face open. Then learn to work the hook down to a five yard draw. Hit and adjust and hit and adjust and have lots of fun. Forget about trying to hit the ball straight. The level of precision required to hit the ball straight is phenomenal. Even the great Ben Hogan said that if he ever hit a ball straight, it was an accident.

ROTATED AT IMPACT

The loft on short irons imparts more back-spin than side-spin to the ball, which straightens out the ball flight. As such, you won't see much curvature until you get to the 7 iron. As you progress through the longer clubs, you will notice increased curvature due to decreased back-spin, and increased side-spin. Many people think they swing differently with short irons than long irons and woods because the ball flies straighter with the shorter clubs. The fact is, loft lets you get away with swing flaws with short irons, but the long clubs tell the truth about the quality of your swing. For now, do the majority of your practicing with a 7 or 6 iron so that you can see some curvature. When you have success with those clubs, start working with the three wood. Use the Obstacle Course to make sure your path is correct. You can also use the direction of your divot to check your club path. A divot that points straight or slightly to the right is fine.

How to practice golf

Not only do most golfers skip short game practice completely, they spend most of their time practicing with the driver, which hurts their game more than anything. You must divide your practice time between short game and full swing practice. You *should* spend two thirds of your time on short game for maximum improvement because two-thirds of the strokes you take in a round of golf will be either putts, chips, or pitches.

There are two modes of golf practice: Golf Swing mode, and Target Golf mode. These two modes are on absolute opposite sides of the golf spectrum and you must discipline yourself to work in only one mode at a time. A good practice session, however, will include both modes of practice.

When you are in Golf Swing mode, you will work on and evaluate mechanics only. **While working on mechanics, *ignore both contact and ball flight*.** As you've already heard, if you *really* want to learn fast, slow everything down and use some sort of feedback mechanism so that you know you are practicing correctly. Do your drills. Do your Gradual Acceleration drill until you graduate to full speed. Practice with full attention and intention. Know exactly what you intend to accomplish, and pay attention so that you practice precisely.

When you swing the club, don't just swing it around. *Feel* the club head in your hands. Concentrate on increasing your awareness of the club head. Turn your head and watch the club move. Try to bridge the gap between what you **see** the club doing and what you **feel** it is doing.

In the beginning of your golf education, spend seventy-five percent of your time on drills to learn your mechanics. As your mechanics improve, gradually lower that percentage until you spend only about twenty-five percent of your practice time drilling. After you've put in your time drilling, go on to ball flight control practice, which I have included under Golf Swing practice, although it is the link between the two modes. In ball flight control practice, work on your **club path** and **face angle** to create a draw. Educate your hands. Teach yourself to create any kind of shot you want. You will eventually need to be able to make the ball curve in both directions, so go ahead and play around. See what you can make the ball do and have fun. It's really neat to be able to control the ball, and when you can control the ball, you are ready for Target Golf.

Alignment

Alignment is critical. You must know where you are aiming before you can accurately evaluate your ball flight. Lay down a club parallel to the target line to help yourself align correctly every time. Imagine train tracks running to the target—your feet go on one track and the ball goes on the other. Always practice with an alignment club. Alignment is one of the easiest fundamentals to get right, and *the* easiest to get wrong. You can ruin you swing in just one practice session if your alignment is off.

OK, good alignment is now a given, and you can now work on getting the ball to the target by going through your pre-shot routine *every time you try to hit a ball to a target, for the rest of your life!!!*

When in Target Golf mode, use your pre-shot routine, and concentrate only on sending the ball to the target. Whether that means the actual target, the Arc of Approach, or the adjusted target. It's pretty simple, folks. Practice picking out a target and concentrating solely on that target (whatever it is) while you swing, just as you will need to do on the golf course. Target Golf requires that you trust your swing, in whatever state of repair it is, regardless of whether you still have things to work on. Forgetting your mechanics takes practice, too, so make sure that you spend ample practice time just focusing on swing to the target. Forget about how to swing, focus on where to swing.

Target Golf practice is just like playing a round of golf on the range. Practicing in this way will greatly help you bring your best golf to the golf course. You may know a few people who are what I call "Range Pros." They look great on the range, but fall apart on the course. These folks just need to change the way they practice to greatly improve their game. The Pre-Shot routine is the key to getting your mind focused on the task at hand, so that you give yourself the opportunity to play your best golf. That's all you can ask of yourself.

THE ADJUSTED TARGET

I have found it astoundingly successful to have my students aim and align to their *actual* target, and then pick out an *adjusted*, or secondary, target to which they will swing the club. To get the ball to the actual target, the adjusted target very often needs to be well right of the actual, because feel is not real. Sometimes you have to fool yourself into swinging toward the actual target by *feeling* like you are swinging way right of it. Wow, does this idea work wonders for many students!

PRE-SHOT ROUTINE, PART 2

We have already discussed the Pre-Shot Routine, but I'd like to get a little deeper into it now. As I have said, before you hit a golf ball, you will want to preprogram your brain for success by going through the three steps that make up the pre-shot routine.

First, SEE the shot you are trying to hit. Visualize the flight of the ball, including how the wind will affect the shot and the way the ball will bounce and roll to the target, or into the hole.

Second, FEEL the swing which makes the ball go to the target. This stage is up to you. Sometimes you will need several rehearsal swings to get the right feel, and sometimes you may need only one. Do not get into the habit of taking the same number of swings each time just to make your routine the same each time. Take rehearsal swings until your brain tells you you're ready. Remember the difference between practice and rehearsal—don't practice your mechanics, feel your swing.

Third, look at your target to lock it in mind, then look back to the ball and then DO IT. If you want the ball to go to the target, you must commit yourself to the shot you are on by swinging with only the target in mind. That goes for every shot you hit. Your mind needs to be focused on one thing in order to function at its potential. What better object to focus on than the target? When you have swing thoughts in your mind, you are not focused on the target. Save swing thoughts for Golf Swing practice. When you have a target to get to, you need to trust what you've trained and swing freely toward the target you have in mind. As I've said, you can focus on the actual target, the adjusted target, or the Arc of Approach.

After you hit the shot, smile if you've hit it well. Tell yourself "That's a goodie!" If you've gotten an undesirable result, immediately make a perfect practice swing and tell yourself "That's the right swing!" When you make this **review swing**, imagine the ball flying right where you wanted it to go. Get a positive charge from your review swing just as if you had actually hit the shot that way. Your brain stores whatever you give more emotion to, so give emotion only to results you want to store. Don't let undesirable results bug you. That only makes them stand out in your mind, and you don't want that, do you?

It's like programming a computer. Your pre-shot routine is programming your brain for success. Your post-shot (review) swing is a way of reprogramming yourself after a less desirable outcome. It helps to put a bad swing out of your mind fast, and replace it with a good swing. For every shot, do the Three R's; Rehearsal Swing, Real Swing, and Review swing.

Anxiety comes from a "results oriented" approach to the game: "don't mess this up" or "don't look like a fool" and etc. The pre-shot routine will help you maintain a "process orientation that will help you forget about "what if I miss?"

Incidentally, don't forget what I said earlier about waggling the club (mini-previews of the Arc of Approach) before you swing. They help you calm down.

RECOMMENDED PRACTICE ROUTINE

You may not be able to practice every day, but whenever you do get to practice, do it this way and you'll improve fast. Get to the putting green and begin your putting drills. Start with ten in a row from two feet and then ten more from three feet. Do the Around the World drill from three feet. Do the Four Corners drill from three paces away. Do the Twenty Footer drill, and then do the Three Ball drill and the Ladder drill until you feel good about your distance control. Play games against a friend if you can to make it more fun and more like the real thing.

Move on to chipping with your sand wedge, and finish chipping practice with the Up and Down Game. Don't go on until you get at least five up and down. As you improve, set the number higher. (You don't have to get them all in a row, by the way.)

Next, head to the range and warm up your full swing with a pitching game I call Leap Frog. With a sand wedge, hit a five yard pitch shot, and note where the ball comes to rest. Try to land the next ball on top of the previous one. Continue the process until you reach full swing. Not only will you have a slow and thorough warm-up, but you will also practice one of the most important scoring skills you need.

After you finish warming up, go to the full swing with your 7 iron, and do the Gradual Acceleration drill, starting at 50 yds and progressing by 25 yds until you reach full speed. Make sure you *graduate* to full speed, don't skip right to it. Once that's done, it's time to forget about mechanics and send the ball to a target.

Start with sand wedge again and work on accuracy. Don't use another club until you are satisfied with your results. Make a goal of so many balls on the green or within a certain area before you change clubs, and work your way up through your set. A goal of just two or three good shots is fine for now. You can increase that number as you improve. Spend most of your time *hitting golf shots* with your 6, 7, 8, and 9 irons, and your wedges. Spend a little time on long irons, but don't overdo it. Of all the long clubs, spend the most time with your 3 wood, because it will probably be your most reliable club when you really need to get the ball in play off the tee.

Long irons and the driver may make you get real fast with your tempo if you try to press for distance. You do not need to swing any harder to hit the ball farther with longer clubs. Your clubs are designed with different length shafts and different lofts to automatically hit the ball different distances. The only thing you need to change is how far apart you set your feet at address. Your clubs will even tell you how far to stand from the ball. You just have to let your arms hang down loosely at address. Let the clubs do the work.

Find a friend at the range and play closest to the pin contests to make practice more fun and meaningful. Play golf on the range. Imagine the holes at your golf course, and play a few holes from tee to green. Go through your routine and hit a drive.

Switch clubs and hit an iron. Imagine long holes and short holes. Realize that in golf, you will seldom get to use the same club twice in a row. You need to practice switching between clubs. Use your imagination. Do anything you can to make practice more realistic and more fun.

Remember, this is supposed to be fun. Whenever you have a club in your hands, it is better to think that you are playing, not working.

THE ART OF PRACTICING

Note the two alignment clubs on the ground by my feet. Imagine a set of train tracks going toward the target. Your feet go on the inside rail, and the ball-to-target line is on the outside rail, making your stance line (line across your toes) parallel to the target line. Make certain that you are properly aligned to the target, only then can you work on your ball flight control.

AVOID THE "FIX IT" MENTALITY

Don't try to fix the last swing. It's too late, not to mention unnecessary. Do you know what your good swing is? I should hope so by now! If you do, you never need to fix anything. You just have to replace your errant swings with your good swing and carry on.

A lot of golfers waste a lot of mental energy trying to figure out what's wrong with their swing during a round of golf. The fact is, you have no way of knowing whether you are actually making a mechanical error, aiming or aligning poorly, or simply experiencing brain interference rather than focusing on the target. Swings don't break down. Something we do in the process of swinging is where we go wrong.

USING VIDEO TAPE

As you know, I highly recommend using good feedback, and video is the best. When shooting the target line view, set the camera so that it is parallel to the target line, and your right shoulder is in the center of the lens. If you don't get the camera parallel to the target line, your view will be inaccurate. For the facing view, make sure the camera lens is perpendicular to the target line, and that you are centered in the lens. The other angles shown in this book are good for illustration, but you'll need to use the facing view, and the target line view for yourself. I'll usually tape three or four swings, then look at them, and then go back and tape three or four more with the necessary adjustment. Keep trying until you see the club moving in the right direction. Look for the club shaft in-line with the right forearm if you're having ball flight control problems. Look for your arms' extension through impact if you're having contact problems. Try to work on just one thing at a time, it's much easier on your brain.

RHYTHM AND TEMPO

A golf instruction book would be incomplete without some mention of rhythm and tempo. While it's difficult to distinguish between the two, they are not the same. Rhythm can be defined as how fast your backswing is relative to your downswing, while tempo can be defined as the overall speed of your swing.

Your swing is rhythmic when your backswing and downswing take the same amount of time, just like a pendulum. Think of the beat of a metronome when trying to assess your rhythm and tempo. In fact, go buy a metronome right now and train your rhythm by using it (or saying "back—through") as you swing. Find a tempo (overall speed) that feels comfortable—not too fast, not too slow—and swing the club back and through right along with the beat: back on one beat, forward on the next. Try slower and faster tempos while maintaining your rhythm and you'll soon find your ideal tempo. Try humming while you swing and listen to what happens to the note you're humming on the downswing: you can learn a lot about your rhythm.

Once you find your rhythm, try switching clubs using the exact same rhythm and tempo. This is much more difficult than it sounds, but if you watch a tour golfer, you'll find that every club is swung with the same rhythm and tempo. That's part of what makes them look so good. Rhythm is the glue of your golf game. Athletes from all sports speak of having found their rhythm after a great performance. Often, when your game starts to fall apart, lack of rhythm is the cause, not your swing.

While there are probably as many different tempos as there are different golfers, it no great golfer has poor rhythm. That said, it is best to have a rhythmic swing with a tempo that feels really good to you. The act of swinging a golf club should feel really good, not like you're lifting weights. Sometimes you have to force yourself to make this game look easy. You want to have an overall attitude of calm confidence when you hit the ball, and I assure you that rushing into the shot is no way to cultivate that attitude.

It is true that someone who talks fast, walks fast, eats fast, etc. will probably have a quicker tempo than someone who naturally does the same things slowly, but both swings can have great rhythm. I do think that there should be no hurry to get the shot over with. Let me put it this way. I rarely see anyone swing too slowly, but I regularly see people swing as though they have somewhere else to be.

There are some wonderful players whose rhythm and tempo you would do well to imitate. Davis Love, Nick Faldo, Phil Mickelson, Fred Couples and Ernie Els are great players to emulate. You can also watch just about any of the LPGA players. They bring new meaning to the word smooth.

8
DIFFERENT LIES

The "lie" refers to the way your ball sits on the ground (or elsewhere). One of the inevitabilities of golf is that your ball will come to rest in a very different lie than you will find on the driving range. To become a real golfer, you need to learn how to handle these somewhat more challenging shots, so practice them out on the course whenever you have a chance. Different lies include downhill, uphill, sidehill (below your feet or above your feet), in rough, on a bare spot, and sand shots (and "I hit my drive 320 on #8 today."). There's not really much to them. They may be more challenging, but not much. And, believe it or not, sand play is easy once you get the hang of it!

DOWNHILL

When your ball comes to rest on a downhill slope, you must realize that the ball is going to fly lower than normal and tend to curve to the right.

Take several practice swings in as similar a lie as your ball is in (to the side of the ball or in front or behind it) and note where the club hits the ground. These practice swings will give you an idea of where to position the ball in your stance (probably a little back).

When addressing the ball, get as comfortable with the lie as possible. Don't fight the slope. Allow your weight to be more on your front foot at address, and try to feel as solid and balanced as possible. Don't hit the ball until you are quite comfortable with your stance.

This shot will probably want to curve to the right on you, so you may want to aim a little left to allow for the curve. The ball will also fly lower and "hotter" than normal, so you may want to use a more lofted club than the one you'd normally hit. If it's a normal 8 iron shot, you may want to hit a 9 iron instead.

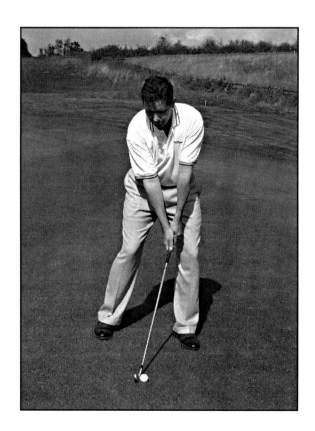

UPHILL

Take your practice swings and get comfortable as before. Move the ball a little forward in your stance to avoid digging into the hill, and try to sweep the ball up the slope. Once again, don't fight the slope, let it tell your body how to relax into address.

This ball will fly higher and shorter than normal, so you should use a less lofted club to cover the required distance. The ball will also tend to curve to the left on you. Adjust your aim appropriately.

BALANCE IS THE KEY

Get as comfortable as you can on all "different lies," and swing well within yourself to maintain balance through the swing.

Sidehill, above your feet

Hold down lower on the grip a little or a lot, relative to how much the ball is above your feet. The higher the ball, the lower you hold. Place the ball in the middle of your stance. Take some practice swings and get comfortable. Sound familiar? This ball will want to curve to the left (hook) on you. The more severe the lie, the more the ball will hook. Aim accordingly to the right.

Sidehill, below your feet

Again, take some practice swings and get comfortable. Place ball location in the middle and get ready for the ball to curve to the right on you. The more severe the lie, the more the ball will fade on you, so adjust your aim.

DEEP ROUGH

There is deep rough and short rough, and the ball can be buried or sitting up. You have to be able to "read the rough" as you would a putting green.

In deep rough, the club will tend to get caught in the grass, forcing the club face to close, very often sending the ball left of the target. If the ball is sitting down, buried in thick grass, use a more lofted club, perhaps only enough club to get safely back into the fairway and avoid more trouble, and allow for the ball to go left. You may want to hold on more tightly through impact to keep the club face from closing down severely. One of the best ways to get out of the rough is to swing the club downward and at the ball rather than along the Arc, creating a more vertical attack. Try to hold the club face a little open through impact and hit an intentional fade.

DEEP ROUGH

SHORT ROUGH

In short rough the ball may fly farther than normal due to grass getting between the ball and club face. You will hear the term "flier lie" often on TV golf telecasts. The flier is hard to predict because the ball seems to "jump" out of light rough and fly farther than normal. The reason why is that grass comes between the ball and the club face at impact, resulting in less backspin and less sidespin. Less backspin means the ball will tend to roll more than usual once it hits the ground. You will want to land the ball short of the target and let it run up. Less sidespin means the ball will also fly quite straight, so don't expect much curve. You are best off to figure out whether you'd rather be short or long, and then play accordingly. Take a look at the target and determine where the trouble is. Choose the club which will be sure to avoid the worst trouble.

FLIER LIE

Tight Lies

A "tight" lie (aka. "bare" lie) has little or no grass around or beneath the ball. The ball will fly lower and "hotter" than normal, so use one less club. No other adjustment need be done other than possibly moving the ball location a little farther back in your stance. Don't let this lie bother you. It is no more difficult than a ball sitting on good fairway grass. You always hit the ball first anyway, right?

In a Divot

As far as I'm concerned, this should never happen, at least not when your ball is in the fairway. I think the rules of golf should allow relief from such a lie. You shouldn't have to pay for some person's lack of consideration. So, if you are not playing in a tournament, move the ball out of the divot—you can seriously injure yourself. If you want, or need, to leave the ball in the divot, just play the ball back in your stance and get ready for a heavy thud at impact. This ball will fly very low, and probably shorter than normal.

SAND PLAY

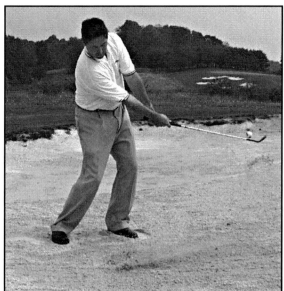

THE SAME MOVE

Notice my arms: just as in every other swing, they are straight as a result of pushing the club down through impact. Every shot has the same move through impact.

Sand play is surprisingly easy once you learn how it's done. There are two types of bunkers, green-side and fairway, and they require completely different techniques. In a green-side bunker, you will contact the sand rather than the ball, and let the sand "push" the ball out. In a fairway bunker, you must contact the ball first, as usual. We'll start with green-side bunkers.

There are two different shots used to get the ball out of green-side bunkers. For good lies, where the ball is sitting nicely on top of the sand, you will slide the club under the ball with a shallow divot: a "slider." When the ball is buried in the sand, in a foot print, or in a depression, you will blast the ball out with a deep divot: an "explosion."

THE SLIDER

For the Slider, position the ball just slightly to the left of center. Open the club face to make use of your sand wedge's "bounce" sole, which is designed to slide through the sand without digging. Align your stance to the left of the target to allow for the open club face, splitting the difference between how far right you aim the club face. For instance, if you aim the club face five yards right of the target, align your stance five yards to the left. The net effect is that the ball will go straight to the target. Dig your feet down into the sand to give yourself firm footing. Put your weight mainly on your left foot.

Make a normal swing and try to enter the sand three inches behind the ball with the objective of throwing the sand out and onto the green. The ball will "ride" the sand to the green. Make sure you swing through impact. Don't let the sand stop you from finishing your swing. If you find that your club stops at impact, you are probably going too deep and taking too much sand.

To vary distances, shorten or lengthen your swing, and possibly vary the speed of your swing. For longer shots use a longer backswing, and do just the opposite for shorter shots. Whatever you do, always accelerate through impact.

You may want to start out with a simple Three Quarter Backswing at first, as you get used to hitting the sand instead of the ball.

Remember: You don't even have to hit the ball. How hard could this be?!

Getting out of bunkers is easy, it just takes a little understanding of the technique involved and some practice. The main objective of your practice is to get used to opening the club face and to work out how deep into the sand you need the club to go and where to enter the sand to get the ball out.

To summarize:
- Ball location **left** of center.
- Align your stance **left** of the target.
- Set your weight firmly on your **left** foot.

} **Remember: Triple Left Setup**

Then:
- Dig your feet in.
- Accelerate through the sand.
- Swing to a full finish.

DRILL

THE RAKE LINE

This drill does not require a ball. In a practice bunker, rake a straight line that is about ten feet long. Then use the butt end of the rake to draw a small line, centered along the length of your big (raked) line. Start at the left end of the line, and swing at the small line. Try to remove equal amounts of sand from both sides of the line, but keep your divot within the big line.

Experiment with short and long swings, with the club face open and closed, and with the depth of the divot you take to get a feel for how to change the distance you would hit a ball.

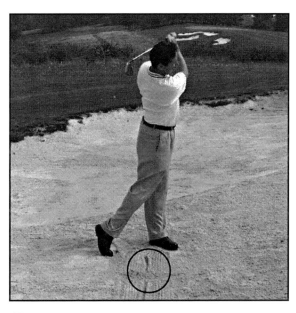

EASIEST PART OF THE GAME

Every other part of golf requires nearly perfect contact to hit good shots. Bunker shots allow you far more room for error. You must experiment to find how far behind the ball you need to hit and how deep into the sand you have to swing to hit good shots. Remember. You must accelerate through contact!

DRILL

Where to Enter the Sand

After you become comfortable with taking sand, put a ball down and with the club head, draw a line in the sand, four inches behind the ball. Try to hit the line first on your way under the ball. If you feel that contact with the sand is stopping you from finishing your swing, you are probably hitting too low beneath the ball, taking too much of a divot. I know it may sound a little too simple, but it really is just a matter of adjusting your swing, either lower or higher, until you find what works. Let the sand do the work!

By the way, want to know how to hit a nice, high, soft pitch shot from either the fairway or the rough? Address the ball just as with a slider (ball location slightly ahead of center, open club face), use your regular pitching motion and hit the ball first. It's fun!

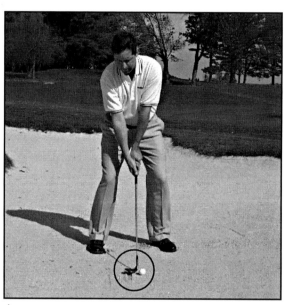

A day at the beach

Note my address position, particularly the club face angle. My stance is left of the target, and my club face is well right of (open to) the target. Once you are comfortable with sand play setup, get into a bunker and hit a bunch of shots. Play in the sand. You'll improve very quickly and get a good tan.

THE EXPLOSION

When the ball is sitting down in the sand, buried, or very close to the front edge of a bunker, you will need to blast it out forcefully. The setup is the same as for the slider, but do not open the club face. Square the club face, and it will dig into the sand for you.

Don't be afraid to swing down forcefully, you are going to have to move a lot of sand to get the ball out of the bunker. And don't be surprised if you are unable to finish your swing.

Practice bunker shots from every kind of lie you can think of. Put the ball in a foot print, a divot, step on it, throw it into the sand so that it looks like a "fried egg," and see what happens, you'll be way ahead of the game.

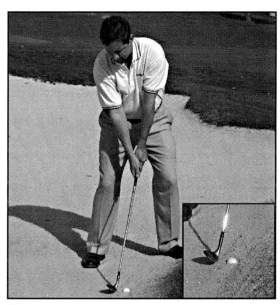

PLAY AT LEARNING

It's easy to turn golf into work. Don't do it. Choose to have fun, and choose to approach learning the game just as a child would. You'll learn faster, and golf won't be an additional source of frustration for you (you probably have enough already).

FAIRWAY BUNKERS

Fairway bunkers require a different strategy, but are not really all that difficult to play from if you assess the lie properly and play accordingly. The first job is to check the lie of the ball. Is it sitting up on top of the sand, or is sand behind the ball? Sand behind the ball will make it impossible to contact the ball first. Is the edge of the bunker much higher than the ball? And how close to the edge is the ball?

If the edge of the bunker is high, or the ball is sitting down, take out a sand wedge and hit a normal sand shot out safely into play. If you have a good lie, make sure you use a club with enough loft to clear the edge of the bunker and do this:

- Play the ball just left of center.

- Dig your feet in just a little.

- Make your feet and legs feel dead.

- Take the club back slowly and try to hit the ball first.

Remember. You always hit the ball first anyway, so this is no big deal. The ball may tend to fade on you, so aim a little left. Also use a longer club than you would normally use for that distance and swing easier so that you can keep your balance better.

PLAY SMART
Play conservatively on fairway bunker shots, and avoid trying to pull off a spectacular shot, because if the club hits the sand first, the ball won't go very far at all. Be aggressive with your swing, but choose your target wisely. By the way, that's a good strategy for the entire game.

9
PLAYING GOLF

Well, here we are, ready to play. By now, you have considerable high-quality practice time behind you on all aspects of the game, and you have much more than just an understanding of the mechanics of the short game and full swing. You are now ready to apply your knowledge.

You should be reasonably confident in your ability to send the ball near the target before you attempt a busy, full size golf course. I don't mean to say that you should be shooting par already, but if you are hitting the ball sideways, you are not ready for the golf course. That may sound harsh, but it's true. If you go on the course before you are ready, you're going to find out how difficult this game can be. I'm trying to help you avoid that.

Before you do golf your ball, however, there are a few things you should know. This chapter will give you everything you need to know about playing golf. We'll start with etiquette, and then move onto the game.

ETIQUETTE

I'm no Emily Post, but there are a few things you need to know before you go on the course. Not knowing golf's protocol can be quite embarrassing if you are playing with other golfers, especially golfers you don't know. All it takes to look like you belong on a golf course is a little awareness and consideration.

WHAT TO WEAR

Men wear collared shirts and pants or Bermuda shorts. Golf shoes really help, and give you much more support than running shoes or tennis shoes. No T-shirts or denims. Women may wear skirts, shorts or pants and golf shirts. Some clubs allow women to wear sleeveless shirts. Golf is an elegant game, and we should keep it that way. I wouldn't mind a bit if we still played in our Sunday best. Bring sun screen. You are going to bake out there.

YOUR TEE TIME

Call the pro shop to get a tee time, and don't be surprised if you are asked to give a credit card number over the phone to secure it if you are going to play a busy course. Most courses allow you to make a tee time up to one week in advance, and some don't take walk-ons, so give a call to be sure you can play.

You are supposed to be teeing off at your tee time, not just getting to the course, so arrive at the course at least 15 minutes before your tee time. Get there an hour early if you can. An hour will give you time to stretch a little, hit a few range balls, and get in a little putting and chipping practice. This warm-up time is a whole lot better for your score than using the first few holes to warm-up.

WHERE TO STAND

When others in your group are playing, you should stand so that you face the golfer whenever possible. When others are teeing off, you may stand behind them so that you have their ball and the target in line to help them see their ball. I often have a player in my group watch my shot this way when I'm playing into the sun. Some players don't like anyone to stand behind them at all, so ask first.

Other than on the tee shot, you may stand slightly ahead and to the side of other players, but not so much that you distract them or put yourself in danger of a stray shot. The best way to find out what distracts people is to ask. You want to get to your ball as quickly as possible, but you don't want to bother the others in your group. I sometimes see all the players in a group waiting behind one player while he hits, and then they all move to the next ball and so on, in a really slow parade around the golf course. Carts can actually slow down play when players wait at each others ball. Drop your rider off at his/her ball and then go to your ball. Don't wait. The key to keeping play moving is to be as near your ball as possible, so that you may play your shot as soon as it is your turn.

Two big No, No's are walking and talking while others are hitting. When a player takes his/her stance, there should be no talking and no distracting movement.

WHO GOES FIRST?

The order of play for the first shot is decided on the first tee by flipping a coin, throwing a tee to see who it points to when it lands, or simply by asking who wants to go first. Unless you are in a tournament, you don't have to be formal.

After the first hole, the player with the lowest score on the previous hole will have the "honor" and will play his/her tee shot first, followed by the player with the next lowest score and so on.

On the rest of the course, including the putting green, the player who is farthest from the hole will play first. When players make the same score on a hole, the order from the previous hole is kept on the next hole.

When in a group where players are playing from different sets of tees, allow those on the more rearward tees to play first.

CARTS

First of all, don't take a cart if you can avoid it. The game is meant for walking. Golf, for many, has turned into a race, with golfers speeding from shot to shot, completely missing the beauty of the sport.

If you are going to use a cart, please obey the signs up on the course that tell you where to drive. There are good reasons why the course superintendent puts up cart travel signs. You will damage either yourself, or the course if you don't follow these signs.

Always keep carts away from the greens. Don't park or drive where you think someone might have to chip or pitch from. If there are cart paths around the greens, use them. It's just consideration. How would you like it if your ball came to rest in a tire track near the green?

SLOW PLAY

Slow play is not pretty but not being a good golfer is not a good reason for being a slow player. Play slows down because players either are not ready to hit when their turn comes, or they spend too much time looking for balls.

Be ready when your turn comes by moving to your ball quickly and lining up your shot while the others in your group are hitting their shots whenever possible. You don't want to walk too far in front of your group because you don't want to distract them or get hit, but if you can get a little ahead, it will help. Most importantly, *be ready when it's your turn!*

This business of looking for balls on the golf course has gotten way out of hand. I know golf balls are expensive but they are not made of gold. If you have to look for a ball, make it quick, and if another group comes up behind you, either move it along, or let them play through.

Agree to play ready golf when you get on the first tee. Ready golf means the first one to their ball plays first.

Some people look for more than their own ball and really slow down play. We call these folks "ball hawks," and they have no place on the golf course, except when no one else is on it (i.e. just about never). Some ball hawks think it's OK to look for balls when they are not playing. They will come to the course and scour the high grass for balls while others are playing. This practice is wrong and should be disallowed totally. It is distracting to players and unsafe for the ball hawks.

When you lose a ball

You are going to lose a ball at some point in your career. You might lose a lot of them. When you hit a shot that you don't think you will find, and the ball did not go into a **water hazard**, the proper procedure is to play a **provisional ball**, as allowed in the rules. If you think you might have lost your tee shot, wait for the others to tee off, and then announce that you are going to play a provisional ball and do so. A provisional ball doesn't count until you decide that you can't find your original ball.

If, after a brief search (two minutes, max.), you come up empty, play your provisional ball. You must count the original shot and the provisional shot, and add a penalty stroke and resume counting your strokes as normal. The provisional ball option may be applied to balls lost from any position on the course, except for a ball lost in a water hazard.

A ball lost in a water hazard is different. You may *not* play a provisional ball in this case. You may reload from the tee, or drop another ball as near to the spot from which you played the previous ball and add a stroke penalty, (the only time you *should* do so is when the hazard is right in front of you). Otherwise, you should drop a ball within two club lengths of where the ball last crossed the hazard's margin, and play from there with a one stroke penalty.

The Rules of Golf book is not really meant for the casual golfer to read and understand, but there is a book called *Golf Rules in Pictures* by Tom Watson and the USGA (United Stated Golf Association) that is very worth reading.

On the putting green

The putting green is sacred ground. You must be careful not to walk on anyone's line to the hole. That may be the biggest No-No in golf. You may step over the line or walk around it to avoid the evil eye.

When your ball is close to anyone's line of putt, you should mark it with a coin or other small object. When your marker is directly in someone's way, you may move it one or more putter head lengths to the side, and then return it after they putt. When moving your marker, use a tree or some other object to move it toward so that you may accurately replace it.

When a player has a long putt, you may be asked to "attend" the flag stick (often called "tend"). To mark the hole for the other player, you should stand as far from the hole as possible and so that your shadow does not cover the hole while you hold the flag stick. Also, hold the flag, itself, so that it does not blow in the wind. After the ball is struck, pull out the flag stick so that the ball does not hit it. Then place the flag stick on the fringe, out of everyone's way.

MARKING A BALL

Place your bag near the green, but never on it, and out of the way of everyone's line of play. Preferably place it so that it is on your way to the next tee.

Try to line up your putts as much as you can while the others are putting so that you are ready when it's your turn. However, do not move around while they are standing over the ball ready to putt.

Please be careful when walking on the greens. Some people (inadvertently, I hope) drag their feet or twist their spikes in the green as they walk, and really damage the putting surface. Never run on a putting green.

MAINTAINING THE COURSE

True golfers keep the course in good condition for those behind them. Fix your divots in the fairways and on tees either by be replacing them, or filling them with sand/seed mix, depending on the preferred method at that course. Repair ball marks on the green and fringe by using a tee or ball mark repair tool. Pull back the pushed-up part, then lift around the indentation to make it more level. Finally, tap with the sole of your putter to even it off. Make it as flat as possible. You may even want to fix more than one just because you care. Rake your footprints and divots in bunkers. There is nothing more annoying than to hit your ball into a bunker and then find it in some jerk's footprint. Some clubs differ in their policy, but it is a good idea to place the rake in the bunker when you are through.

Sometimes you will see a little box at par three holes. It's not a trash can. This box is filled with a sand/seed mixture that is used to fill divots. Fill yours and another.

PLAYING THROUGH

You may find that your group is holding up play and backing up the course. When there is no one on the hole in front of you, you are playing too slowly. When there is a hole open in front of you and there is a group right behind waiting for you to get out of the way, it's time to allow them to play through.

The same deal applies when you are being held up and there is a hole open in front of the group ahead of you. They should allow you to play through, but sometimes they don't for one reason or another. You may want to tactfully ask them *after* you find out for certain that there is a hole open ahead of them.

There really isn't much more to golf's etiquette than that. It's pretty much common sense and decency. Just be aware of the other people around (and not only those in your group), keep moving, and keep the course in the condition you want it to be in and you'll be just fine. Oh, one more thing. Turn off your cellular phone and don't use it on the golf course. Better yet, don't even bring it with you.

You don't have to be embarrassed about how well you play, most people aren't much better than you anyway, but when you fail to observe the etiquette of the game, that's embarrassing.

GOLF: THE MIND GAME

Finally, after all that, we come to what you really wanted to know: How to play golf. You have learned the techniques of the full swing and the short game and how to apply them to the different conditions you'll find on the golf course. Now you are ready to use what you have learned on the course. Here, we will consider the real game: how to think on the course.

Everything you have learned so far has been easy. The difficult part of golf is between your ears. You need to put your brain in gear to give yourself the best possible chance to score well. There is a wealth of literature on the psychology of golf, and while I am no psychologist, I can tell you what I think are the basics of golf psychology.

Basically, you are in total control of what you think. Your job is simply to put your brain in the right place on every shot. Sounds easy. Actually, I could end this discussion right here, because there really is nothing more to the game. Missed shots are more a result of poor preparation or poor attention than poor technique. If you want good results, concentrate on the shot you are about to hit (in the present), not on what just happened (in the past), or what might happen (in the future). You can't do anything about the shot you just hit, you can only give yourself the best possible chance of success on the shot you are faced with. The way to give yourself the best chance is to go through your routine every time and make sure that you commit to the shot you are hitting. You are committed to the shot only when you have nothing but the target in mind when you swing. Think of throwing a dart. You never think of how to throw it, you just look at the target and throw. Do the same on the golf course.

Some golfers work on their swing on the range and then go to the golf course and work on it some more. I appreciate the desire to improve their swing that these players have, but please understand that it is more important that you learn how to focus your attention solely on sending the ball to the target and forget all about how to swing, even if your swing still needs work. Save work for the range. *Play* when you play. More accurately, hit golf shots to targets. Don't think about how to swing the club, think "where's my target," and swing the club toward it. Just watch the tour players. There are a lot of them who have less than perfect swings, but they still manage to shoot low scores.

The ability to commit to the shot at hand is the most important skill you will develop in your quest for lower scores. Let me tell you, it's hard to let go of those technical thoughts that run through your mind as you try to swing the club. You will have to practice it on the range. Don't wait until you get to the course to try it. You need to practice *playing* (committing to the shot and trusting yourself) on the range. Think about it. If you focus your attention on swing mechanics, doesn't that automatically make it impossible to focus your attention on the target? Golf is a target game. Don't ever forget that. Train your golf swing at the range, and trust what you've trained as soon as you step on the course. And, of course, practice trusting your swing at the range too. The same applies to the short game, as well.

Realize that, no matter how good you get, you will always hit some strange looking golf shots. Don't try to fix those shots on the golf course. Just let them go. So many golfers try to fix their swing, only to have the wheels come completely off. The reason is that the more mechanical they become, the farther away their attention goes from the target. After you hit one of those weird ones, take a practice swing or two to remind yourself of what you had intended to do, accept the shot, and go on to the next. The secret of golf psychology is to force yourself to think properly. You must forget about the shot you just hit in order to prepare yourself for the shot you are about to hit. Your pre-shot routine is designed to help you do just that, so stick to your pre-shot routine.

Whenever you hit a shot that is playable, count it as a good shot. Avoid perfectionism. You'll seldom see the best golfers in the world hit perfect shots. So when you hit a "good enough" shot, don't analyze why it didn't fly *exactly* as you had hoped. If you can find the ball after you've hit it, that's good enough. Go hit it again. Don't get too excited about bad shots. Thinking about the shot you just missed is living in the past, and does not help you hit the next shot at all.

My own experience playing golf has led to an important self-discovery. It seems as though there are key moments during a round of golf where I have to make a decision as to how I will react to a missed shot. Those times when I have allowed myself to get angry have often led to an overall negative attitude throughout the round. Although I have often been able to recover and play good golf, the times when I have chosen to get angry have often ruined my whole day, and that's just not good.

However, on the days when I have forced myself to accept missed shots and just moved on to the next shot, regardless of my score, I have *always* managed to have a good day. Thinking properly does not always mean that I play well, but at least the bad round doesn't come home with me.

The least I can say after a round where I have thought properly is that I gave myself the best chance to play well that I could. The best you can do is the best you can do, so don't panic.

Lower scores are not the only goal in golf, you know. Some people are happy just to be on the course and could care less what they shoot. These people may have the right idea. Playing golf just for the fun of it will loosen you up. You will hit more good shots if you don't have the self-imposed pressure to hit every shot well. *Try* to hit every shot perfectly, but don't *expect* to.

Some of us work hard at the game and feel we deserve to play better. We get frustrated when we shoot higher scores than we are capable of, because we feel that we *should* play better. Chuck Hogan, one of the best golf coaches in the world and someone I admire greatly, used to wear a shirt that had the message, "Don't **should** on Me" printed on it. I think I'm going to get one of those. We need to learn to give ourselves the best possible chance to score well and be happy with that. Golf is difficult, unpredictable and can be maddening if you look at your results rather than at the *process* of golfing your ball.

The process of golfing requires that you focus your attention. Playing your best requires a good pre-shot routine, confidence, commitment, and composure.

PRE-SHOT ROUTINE

Your pre-shot routine is, when it comes to actually playing golf, the most important weapon in your bag. Although we have discussed it many times before, I feel that it is worth mentioning yet again. Your routine puts your mind in focus for the task at hand.

1 SEE IT

2 FEEL IT

3 DO IT

LISTEN. We've been over this before. If you want to play well, don't put Step Three ahead of Step One and Step Two.

Before you get to Step One, you must go through a situation assessment in which you will check your lie, the wind, locate trouble and use these factors to help you select a target. Begin this assessment as you walk to the ball, and finalize it when you get there.

STEP ONE: SEE IT

Visualization is a vitally important skill which you can and will improve with practice. See the flight you wish ball to take, including what effect the wind will have on it, and see the way it will bounce and roll to the target. Visualizing helps the mind and body work together. You may do this several times before you actually swing, and the shot you visualize may even help you to choose which club to hit.

This process need not take more than a few seconds, and it will pay big dividends as you focus more clearly on the target and make better shots because of that.

You should visualize all shots from full shots to the shortest putts. It's like playing in your head a movie of your shot before you swing. The great Jack Nicklaus said that he never hit a shot without visualizing first, not even in practice. If it's good enough for Jack, it's good enough for you.

If you find it difficult to see the ball flying high against the sky at first, you may want to see a road in the sky or on the green or anything you can think of. Some players use a train on a track for putting and see the train fall into the hole. Anything that locks you onto the shot will work.

STEP TWO: FEEL IT

Step Two is simple. Feel the swing you need to make to create the shot you have visualized.

Sometimes you will need only one swing to feel it, and sometimes you will need more. The point is, do not hit the ball until you are confident that you are ready. Seeing the shot will automatically trigger a muscular response, feeling the right swing will make it absolutely clear, and then you only have to fix the target in your mind and swing. SEE it and FEEL it until your brain tells you you're ready. *Rehearse* the feel of the shot you want to hit, don't *practice* your mechanics.

STEP THREE: DO IT

Step Three is what many players do as Step One. The problem is that they have done little to give themselves the best possible chance to hit a good shot.

Step Three consists of locking the target in your mind and holding it there while you swing the club. After you address the ball and go through your waggles, look one last time at the target and then slowly move your eyes to the ball. Pause briefly, and then send the ball to the target you have in your mind's eye. Again, this process goes for all shots, from driving to putting. Remember to "Target Lock."

After the shot, rate the quality of your focus on the target on a scale of one to ten. Ten means you were totally focused throughout the swing. One means, "Where am I? What just happened?" Then rate how well you sent your energy toward the target. That's all you consider. Don't worry at all about what went wrong. After an undesirable outcome, take a review practice swing to remind yourself of the right swing, and go on to the next shot. Don't get mechanical when in Target Golf mode. That's the death of a golfer.

ATTENTION AND INTENTION

I ask my students quite often, "What game are you playing, anyway?" I'll stand behind them while we're working on ball flight control and simply watch the path of their club as it moves through impact. When they swing the club left of the target (by far the most common error in golf), I tell them "It didn't look like you had any *intention* to hit the ball to the target." When they swing along the correct Arc of Approach, I tell them "It looked like you *tried* to hit it to the target." Pay *attention* to the target during your entire swing, not just when you address the ball, and swing with the conscious *intention* of sending the ball to the target. You'll be surprised (shocked?) how often you swing without intention.

Many golfers "black out" during the swing, forgetting about everything except the ball. That's why you slice and why the ball doesn't go where you want it to. All I can say is, if you don't pay attention to where you're swinging the club, you're playing the wrong game. Golf's a lot more than just hitting the ball. You have to control where it goes!

COMMITMENT

To "just do it," you need to have your mind clear of all but sending the ball to the target (the shot) to give your brain a chance to focus on the task at hand. The task at hand is to get the ball to the target, not to make a good swing. It is too late for mechanics at this time. Focusing on mechanics will only distract you from your target. Commit to the shot by focusing on it while you swing, and more of your shots will fly there.

Your commitment to golf in general includes regular and intelligent practice in both Golf Swing mode and Target Golf mode. As you improve, you should spend less time on your swing and more time on Target Golf. Also, you should spend at least half of your practice time on your short game. Golf is all about self-discipline. The word discipline originally meant "to lead." Lead yourself in the direction you want to go. If you want to get good, the information is right here for you. You just have to do it. It's that simple.

CONFIDENCE

You must have no doubts in your mind about whether you have the right club, or whether you can get over that water hazard or whatever. Your pre-shot routine will help your confidence because you will see and feel the shot before you hit it, but there is another important matter...

Don't try a shot you don't own. Practice shots on the range before you try them on the course. If you have a 230 yard shot over water to get to the green and you can only hit it 200 yards, don't hit the shot. Lay up to a position from which you can play your next shot to the green. Make every situation as familiar as possible by changing your target to one you know you can hit. When you hit a shot you know you can hit, you'll be more confident and you'll put a better swing on the ball, so stick with your strengths. It is true that you will, at some point, have to try a shot you are unsure of and that's not a bad thing, but you want to keep those times to a minimum. When you try such a shot, you may have doubts in your mind while you swing. The key is to stick to your routine and trust yourself.

ABOUT HAZARDS

Hazards are the golf course architect's tools used to outline the best places to hit your ball. Hazards can cause you to lose confidence, but you can overcome them if you realize that they are only there to help define the target. When you see a hazard, you simply have to notice that it is telling you to pick another place to hit the ball. The more appropriate target may be short of the hazard, over the hazard, or to one side or the other. You must let the hazards define your target for you and then focus on the target. One major difference between good players and not so good players is that not so good players focus on hazards, while good players focus on targets.

COMPOSURE

You will not hit all of your shots perfectly, even if you go through the best routine in the world and have the best swing. You are only human, and as such you will make a bad swing from time to time. The idea is to *put your brain in gear to hit the ball well, and then accept the result and go on to the next shot.* As soon as you allow yourself to

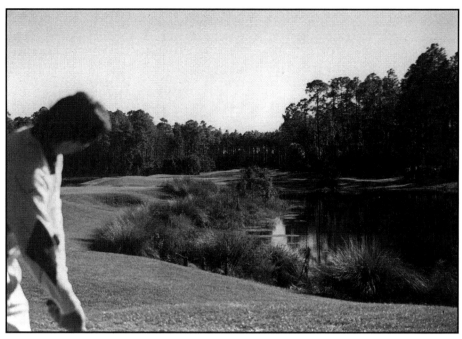

SEE THE TARGET, NOT THE TROUBLE

I love this game! This is where golf becomes fun. Water right, water left, and it's a 580 yd par five. To make the shot, you've got to realize that the water's only there to define the target. Don't get intimidated, just pick your target and forget about the water (unless you *want* the ball to go there). Focus on the shot and swing.

dwell on past shots, you will ruin your chances of playing good golf. These few paragraphs are way too short for the importance of the information they contain. You might want to read them a few more times. Thinking properly sounds so easy, but golf has a way of frustrating people, making them do, think, and say strange things that have little to do with playing good golf.

It helps to realize that one round of golf is not the only measure of your improvement. Even the best players in the world have bad rounds, and they are playing for a living and practicing all day, every day.

Let me get one thing straight. I am not saying you absolutely can't get angry, although it has been found that anger significantly changes your body chemistry for the worse. Composure can be summed up in this statement: Never hit a ball while angry or, in any other way, distracted from focusing on the target. If you hit a ball while thinking, "If I make par here, I'll shoot my best round ever" that's just as bad a mental error as hitting a ball while angry about the previous shot. In both cases, you are not concentrating on the shot at hand, which is the only thing that matters.

I remember playing a round of golf at a really good, challenging golf course in South Carolina. I had been hitting the ball out to the right all day, but had managed enough good shots and holed enough putts to be two under par going into the par five, eighteenth hole.

The ocean lines the right side of the hole and there are several high mounds with bunkers in between the mounds that divide the fairway in two. You can play left or right of the mounds, but you really don't want to be in them. The safe play is left of the mounds, and that's where I had intended to hit my drive, only the ball went right (again) and into the mounds. When I found the ball, it lay in one of the bunkers so that I could not see the golf course at all. I walked up to the top of the mountain of moguls to see where I should hit the ball, walked back to my ball in the bunker, and hit the shot perfectly to the one hundred yard marker.

Now, a one-hundred yard shot is just about my all time favorite. I believe that I can make the shot from there, although I rarely do. But this shot made me wonder a little. The hole was cut in the very front of the green, and the drop-off into the ocean was only about fifteen feet to the right of the hole. I went through my pre-shot routine, settled over the ball and then, just as I was about to hit the ball, "don't hit this to the right" flashed in my mind. Luckily, I had the presence of mind to back away from the ball and take the opportunity to chastise myself for my poor thinking. I reminded myself that I *owned* this shot. I focused on the target, trying to hole the shot, and hit the ball six inches from the cup. I had kept my composure and focused on the shot at hand. And it *worked*. That shot, although it didn't come in a tournament, stands out clearly in my memory because it perfectly illustrates the importance of focusing on the shot at hand.

Composure is simply having the presence of mind to control your thoughts so that you send your brain in the direction you want it to go. Golf seems to lend itself so well to negative thinking because you so seldom hit perfect shots. The playing of golf includes something I call "The Negativity Battle." You have to fight those negative thoughts and stay positive for the next shot. Keep your mind on the shot you are about to hit, not on the one you just hit or what you will do in the near future.

Let's look at few ways I know of to maintain your composure.

Target Lock every shot. Don't swing until your brain tells you you're ready. If you find yourself thinking bad thoughts over the ball, back away and go through your routine again. Wait out bad thoughts until you can replace them with good ones.

If you are overly pumped up, either positively or negatively, tighten up every muscle in your body as much as possible, and then just let go. While you let go, let the last shot go and move on to the next.

Breath deeply in through the nose and out through the mouth, especially just before you swing.

Squeeze the ball tightly and then let go. When you let the ball go, let the last shot go, too.

Tie your shoes.

Smile. Think of something that makes you smile. Try to laugh off bad shots. Your friends will think you're crazy, but they will probably be giving you their money at the end of the round.

Be careful of getting angry. I, personally, find that it seems to escalate if I allow too many negative reactions to results I don't like. You know yourself. If you can blow off a little steam without bothering anyone else and still be fully prepared for the next shot, you're in good shape.

There are days when nothing goes right. I firmly believe that there are days when your body just won't do what you want it to do. On these days, practice thinking the right things. You can always improve your mental game, even if your physical game is off, so take every opportunity to strengthen this most important part of your game.

Do your best by thinking correctly and practicing correctly. Sometimes, your best for that particular day is ten strokes or more higher than what you usually shoot. That's OK, as long as you gave yourself the chance to play your best. "Do your best" does not mean *play* your best. It means give your best effort. Tell that to your kids, please. If you can leave the course or practice range and say you did your best, you can be happy. The best you can do is the best you can do, so don't get too excited. There are more rounds and more tournaments still to come. Every round is not a measure of your improvement. You have to look at progress with a long term view, not from day to day. Keep up your practice, both mental and physical, and keep plugging away. Don't ever give up.

A game of golf begins when you first take up the game and ends when you stop playing for good. Take a long term view of your game. Unfortunately, you will only recognize improvement in retrospect. Let's put it this way. You are on the path to mastery of the game, and the path has no end. You will never master the game, but that's not important. What you *will* do is improve for the rest of your golfing days. The *path* to mastery is where all fun is.

10
TROUBLESHOOTING

This chapter will help you find solutions to problems which may come up as you learn and play golf. Consult it whenever things start to fall apart. Usually, all you will have to do is go back to basics to reaffirm your fundamentals. Don't search for tips and quick fixes. They don't work. And don't listen to friends. The fact is, you now know more about golf than most of the people who play the game and all you'll get is conflicting information and a headache. Reread the appropriate section and make sure you are doing what you are supposed to do. Get yourself on video tape so that you know for sure what's going on. You may have to slow down and retrain. Keep in mind that if you swing the club correctly the ball *has* to go toward the target. You just have to make sure you make the right swing. You know what's right now, and that's a lot better than trying to figure out what you did wrong.

IF YOU FIND THAT YOU OFTEN MISS THE BALL COMPLETELY OR CONSISTENTLY TOP THE BALL:

1. Make sure you are extending your arms back into the Iron Triangle, pushing the club down the Arc through impact.

2. Move closer to the ball and make sure your arms hang straight down from your shoulders. Check address position and balance.

3. Swing lower. Don't be afraid to hit the ground. Adjust. Get the feedback your brain requires by swinging too high sometimes and too low others. Don't allow yourself to make the same mistake twice in a row. If you top the ball on one shot, purposely hit the ground with the next swing. Adjusting equals learning.

4. Swing at the grass, trying to brush it with your club.

5. Practice hitting a tee.

6. Check ball location. It could be too far back in your stance.

7. Make sure you are staying in your posture as you swing, and are not straightening up in your back swing. That's called **maintaining your spine angle**.

IF YOU FIND THAT YOU HIT THE BALL FAT CONSISTENTLY:

1. You may be too close to the ball. Check your address position.

2. Swing higher.

3. Check that your legs are not collapsing on your down swing.

4. Try to keep your spine in the same place while you turn back and through. Maintaining your spine angle is extremely important to your ball striking.

5. Watch for tension in your right shoulder. It may be dropping as you extend your right arm.

IF THE BALL STARTS LEFT AND SLICES:

This happens because your club path is outside-in, and your club face is slightly open at impact. As you know, the outside-in path is caused by a faulty downswing.

1. Check your grip and alignment first.

2. Pick a more appropriate target. Remember the Adjusted Target? You may have to pick a target to the right of the actual target to get yourself to swing in the right direction. Are you swinging the club toward the target?

3. Check overall body tension. Always monitor your tension, it can destroy your swing. Your left hand, in particular, will try to hold on tightly, forcing the club face open at impact.

4. Make sure you start the downswing correctly. If you do not flatten the club shaft as you extent back and down, you cannot swing out toward the target. Make sure those shoulders aren't turning toward the target first.

IF THE BALL STARTS LEFT AND HOOKS:

This problem is similar to the one before. The club path is outside-in, but now the club face is closed at impact, making the ball start left and then curve further left.

1. Check your hold and alignment.

2. Are you keeping the target in mind throughout your swing? Are you sending your energy to the target? Adjust the target farther to the right to send the ball in the right direction.

3. Once you get your swing going in the right direction, then work on your how much you rotate the club face through impact. Educate those hands!

4. Make sure your arms are extending through impact. You may be bending the elbows and pulling the club through impact, rather than pushing it through.

IF THE BALL STARTS RIGHT AND SLICES:

1. Your path is probably good, but your club face is a little open at impact. Make sure you are not "death gripping" the club.

2. Check your grip. The V's should point to your right shoulder. The heel pad of your left hand should be on top of the club.

3. Rotate the club face a little sooner into impact. Basically, your left arm is responsible for rotating the club, so try to roll your left arm over a little earlier. It's similar to making a sharp left turn in a car.

4. Try to get the back of your left hand facing down toward the ground at impact.

5. Try getting your watch to face your left leg at impact.

6. You may have to feel at though club face rotation begins as soon as you start the downswing.

IF YOU SHANK THE BALL:

A **shank** is a shot hit off of the hosel of the club and goes almost straight off to the right. The **hosel** is the part of the club head where the shaft is attached. The only way you can shank a ball is to be too close to it. You may have simply stood too close at address or, during the swing, you moved closer.

1. Stand a little farther from the ball.

2. Check you weight distribution at address. You may be out on the balls of your feet. Your weight should be 70% on your heels.

3. Try to feel whether you are leaning in toward the ball as you swing. The cure for leaning in is to stand tall as you swing and keep your weight on your heels. Don't let your head drop down or drift toward the ball.

4. Try to hit the ball off of the toe of your club, then try to shank it. Train your hands to bring the center of the club face to the ball. My favorite word is "adjust." Adjusting equals learning.

IF YOU CONSISTENTLY LOSE YOUR BALANCE DURING YOUR SWING:

1. Check your weight distribution at address: 70% on your heels.

2. You may be swinging too hard.

3. You may have too much tension in your body during the swing. Try to relax.

4. Make sure that you load your weight onto your right leg on the backswing. You may be straightening your right knee, sending your weight to your left foot at the top of the backswing in what's called a "reverse pivot." Remember that if you turn well and maintain the flex in your right knee as you go back, your weight will *automatically* shift to your right leg.

IF YOU HAVE TROUBLE MAKING SOLID CONTACT WITH CHIPS AND PITCHES:

1. Check your setup. Remember stance left, weight left, shaft left and ball location to the right.

2. Push the club down through impact—arms straightening through impact.

3. Keep your weight on your left foot throughout the stroke.

4. Use the Long Club!

IF YOU HAVE TROUBLE MAKING SOLID, CENTERED CONTACT WITH YOUR FULL SWING:

1. Don't worry too much. Keep making your good swing, and allow your phenomenally intelligent subconscious mind to find the center of the club face for you. You'll hit the ball just fine as soon as you have put in enough practice time.

2. Check setup. Balance is key. Just a slight loss of balance can throw your swing completely off.

3. Check ball location. It should be within two inches of the inside of your left heel.

4. Cover the club face with duct tape to find out exactly where you're making contact.

GOLF YOUR BALL

Now you have the skills necessary to play golf and you know just about everything you need to know. How good you get depends upon how well and how often you practice and how often you play.

Another of my favorite sayings is "Go golf your ball." What I mean by that is go out there and hit the ball, find it, and hit it again until you run out of holes to play. When people ask me how I am playing, I often answer, "I'm golfin' my ball," no matter how well I happen to be playing. Have as much fun as you can. That's the whole point!

Even when you start getting good, continue doing your drills. At least do the ones that work the best for you. The Gradual Acceleration drill is an excellent warm up to use for the rest of your golf career and it helps you maintain your swing.

If possible, video tape yourself while hitting balls in order to see what's *really* happening in your swing. Use the same viewpoints as with the mirrors (down the target line and face on). If you are going to take a lesson, insist on being video taped. You will learn *so* much faster if you can see what you are doing.

If you need to work on contact, simply adjust. If you are topping the ball, adjust. If you are hitting it fat, adjust. It's not rocket science! Contact will come easily. The hard part of golf is shooting low numbers. Making pars and birdies takes some work, but playing golf respectably well is easy. Put your time in and practice well, and you will get better fast.

When you play golf, leave your swing thoughts behind and trust what you have trained. Eventhough you may feel that your swing is a "work in progress," you must trust it, in whatever state it happens to be, if you want to play good golf. Focus on either the target, the Adjusted Target or the Arc of Approach (waggle, please). Don't work on your swing on the golf course if you have any intention of shooting a good score.

Your short game is going to be most important in lowering your score, so spend at least half of your practice time working on putting, chipping, and pitching, with a little time on sand play as well.

I sincerely hope that this book has helped you learn golf, and that I might have been able to help you enjoy your game more than ever. Thank you very much!

Go golf your ball!

OTHER INSTRUCTION MATERIAL BY JOHN DUNIGAN

The Secret of the Golf Swing

and

The Secret of the Golf Swing Video

The complete golf swing as taught by John Dunigan

(cut here and return this portion with your payment)

TO ORDER BOOKS FROM GOLF BETTER PRODUCTIONS:

See your local bookstore, or send check or money order to GOLF BETTER PRODUCTIONS, 317 West Biddle St. Suite 1A West Chester, PA 19380. Please allow four weeks for delivery.

Quantity	Title	Price	US Shipping & Handling	Total
	ESSENTIAL GOLF	$24.95	$5.99	
	The Secret of the Golf Swing	$27.95	$5.99	
	The Secret of the Golf Swing Video	$49.95	$5.99	

Send to:

Name _____

Address_____

_____

Please add me to the GOLF BETTER PRODUCTIONS mailing list ____

GOLF BETTER PRODUCTIONS

West Chester, PA

www.golfbetterproductions.com